MAY 9 1978

JUN 30 1979

DEC 23 1979

DATE DUE

Y0-AUJ-182

M 781.62094
Penguin

PENGUIN BOOKS
AU4
THE PENGUIN AUSTRALIAN SONG BOOK
JOHN MANIFOLD

THE PENGUIN
Australian Song Book

COMPILED BY

John Manifold

EVANSTON PUBLIC LIBRARY
1703 ORRINGTON AVENUE
EVANSTON, ILLINOIS

PENGUIN BOOKS

PENGUIN BOOKS LTD, HARMONDSWORTH, MIDDLESEX, ENGLAND
PENGUIN BOOKS INC, BALTIMORE 11, MARYLAND, U.S.A.
PENGUIN BOOKS PTY LTD, RINGWOOD, VICTORIA, AUSTRALIA

—

First Published 1964
Copyright © Penguin Books Pty Ltd, 1964

—

Printed in Australia for Penguin Books Pty Ltd
at The Griffin Press, Adelaide
Set in Monotype Times

This book is sold subject to the condition that it shall not, by way of trade, be lent, re-sold, hired out, or otherwise disposed of without the publisher's consent, in any form of binding or cover other than that in which it is published

CONTENTS

Acknowledgements — viii
Introduction — ix

1 Seamen and Transports — 1

BOUND FOR SOUTH AUSTRALIA (capstan-chanty)	2
BOUND FOR SOUTH AUSTRALIA (halyard)	3
THE LITTLE FISH	5
MAGGIE MAY	6
TEN THOUSAND MILES AWAY	8
THE GIRL WITH THE BLACK VELVET BAND	10
JIM JONES	12
VAN DIEMEN'S LAND	14
MORETON BAY	16
MORETON BAY (another tune)	17
THE CONVICT MAID	19
THE CATALPA	20
BOTANY BAY	22
MY LAST FAREWELL TO STIRLING	23
THE ISLE DE FRANCE	24

2 Immigrants and Diggers — 29

THE POMMY'S LAMENT	30
SIXTEEN THOUSAND MILES FROM HOME	32
BILLY BARLOW IN AUSTRALIA	34
WITH MY SWAG ALL ON MY SHOULDER (or Denis O'Riley)	36
THE OLD PALMER SONG	38
TAMBAROORA GOLD (two versions)	40
LOOK OUT BELOW!	42
THE MINER	43

3 The Bushrangers — 45

MY NAME IS BEN HALL	47
BOLD JACK DONAHUE	48
BOLD JACK DONAHUE (another version)	50
THE WILD COLONIAL BOY	52
THE WILD COLONIAL BOY another version	53
BALLAD OF BEN HALL'S GANG	55
BALLAD OF BEN HALL'S GANG (another version)	56
FRANK GARDINER	58
THE STREETS OF FORBES	60
THE DEATH OF BEN HALL	62
MY NAME IS EDWARD KELLY	64
NED KELLY'S FAREWELL TO GRETA (two versions)	66
YE SONS OF AUSTRALIA	68
STRINGYBARK CREEK	70
STRINGYBARK CREEK (another version)	71
THE BALLAD OF KELLY'S GANG	73

4 Pastoral Australia — 79

MUSTERING DAY	80	FIVE AND A ZACK	96
THE DYING STOCKMAN	82	THE RAM OF DALBY	97
THE DYING STOCKMAN (another version)	83	EUABALONG BALL	98
THE STOCKMAN'S LAST BED	84	THE STRINGYBARK COCKATOO	100
THE STOCKMAN'S LAST BED (another version)	85	OH, GIVE ME A HUT (THE FREE-SELECTOR)	103
THE OLD BARK HUT	87	THE COCKIES OF BUNGAREE	104
THE OLD BARK HUT (another version)	88	EUMERELLA SHORE	106
THE STATION COOK	90	THE LIMEJUICE TUB (THE WHALERS' RHYME)	108
OLD BLACK ALICE	92	THE INGLEWOOD COCKY (or The New England Cocky)	109
JACKY-JACKY	94		

5 The Nomads — 113

THE QUEENSLAND DROVER (THE OVERLANDER)	114	THE BANKS OF THE CONDAMINE (another version)	132
THE QUEENSLAND DROVER (another version)	115	FLASH JACK FROM GUNDAGAI	134
THE UNION BOY	117	BULLOCKY-O	136
THE RYEBUCK SHEARER	118	THE SHEEPWASHER	138
LADIES OF BRISBANE (THE DROVER'S SONG)	120	BILL THE BULLOCKY	139
LADIES OF BRISBANE (AUGATHELLA STATION)	122	THE OLD BULLOCK DRAY	140
THE DROVER'S DREAM	124	HUMPING OLD BLUEY	142
GOORIANAWA	126	I'VE JUST COME FROM SYDNEY	143
WIDGEGOARA JOE (THE BACKBLOCK SHEARER)	128	THE REEDY LAGOON	144
THE BANKS OF THE CONDAMINE	130	WILD ROVER NO MORE	146

6 The Poets — 151

THE COMMISSIONER	152	THE SHEARER'S DREAM	164
THE BROKEN-DOWN SQUATTER	154	FREEDOM ON THE WALLABY	166
BILLYGOAT OVERLAND	156	THE RABBITER	168
TRAVELLING DOWN THE CASTLEREAGH	158	CANE KILLED ABEL	171
WALTZING MATILDA (The Cowan version)	160	THE DEATH OF NED KELLY	172
WALTZING MATILDA	162	ANDY'S GONE WITH CATTLE	174

Books that give the background 177
Notes for Accompanists 177
Table of Guitar-chords 178
Index of First Lines 179

ACKNOWLEDGEMENTS

I WISH to thank Angus & Robertson Ltd for permission to quote from *Old Bush Songs*, by Stewart and Keesing, the following songs: 'The Catalpa', 'Ten Thousand Miles Away', 'Billy Barlow', 'The Station Cook', and 'Song of the Squatter'. 'The Free Selector' is from *Old Bush Songs*, by A.B. Paterson; 'A Bushman's Song' is from *The Collected Verse of Paterson*; 'Andy's Gone With Cattle' from *The Poetical Works of Henry Lawson*; and 'The Shearer's Dream' is from *The Prose Works of Henry Lawson*, all reprinted by permission of Angus & Robertson Ltd. 'The Billygoat Overland' from *The Animals Noah Forgot*, by A.B. Paterson, is reprinted with the permission of *The Bulletin* and Mrs Paterson. 'Freedom on the Wallaby' is from *The Men Who Made Australia*, by Henry Lawson, reprinted with the permission of the Australasian Book Society. 'Waltzing Matilda' is reprinted with the permission of Allan & Co. Pty Ltd, owners of the world copyright.

I am grateful to all the helpers I have had in compiling this book: To the Federation of Bush Music Groups, Brisbane; the Queensland Folklore Society; the Folklore Society of Victoria; the Victorian Bush Music Club, and the Bush Music Club, Sydney, for permission to use material collected by their members and published in their journals; to the Editor of *The Canon* for permission to reprint material of which he holds the copyright; and to John Bellamy, John Callaghan, Ron Edwards, John Meredith, Bill Scott, and Edgar Waters for comments and advice.

J.S.M.

INTRODUCTION

The first white men to settle Australia were London pickpockets, Irish rick-burners, and poachers from the Midlands, already the inheritors of a long tradition of folk-music. With the Londoners, this tradition was overlaid by professionalism: missing the comforts of the gin-palace and the entertainers of Vauxhall and Cremorne, the townsmen were at a loss. But the boys from the country found colonial conditions little harder than those they had left behind, and were prepared to go on singing in their ancestral way.

The Irish seem to have taken the lead. United by more than their chains, they sang in a whisper the old songs of Ireland. At the risk of flogging or hanging they sang the rebel songs too. The authorities called any criticism of the system 'treason', and punished it as such. But this never quite stopped the Irish from singing, and it never stopped them from making up new, local verses to the old tunes.

The late Dr Dalley-Scarlett held that the new words, having different vowel-sounds from the old ones, exerted a 'pull' on the notes they were married to. Whatever the mechanism of the change may have been, some of the old tunes did change. Variants of many tunes known in Ireland, and in England too, have been sung in Australia for over a century. New tunes in the same ancient idiom arose as well. *Van Diemen's Land* was probably sung by Irish convicts before it was ever sung in Ireland. From mouth to ear and from ear to mouth, not always of the same nationality, both kinds of song spread through the convict settlements; and no amount of flogging could stop them.

As the country was opened up, men could get out of earshot of the overseer once in a way, and sing the 'treason songs' with comparative impunity. They could even sing in chorus; and the chorus that grew up to the ballad of *Bold Jack Donahue* was one that no proclamations could stamp out.

Emancipists and bolters and the pick of the free settlers pushed out into the bush where no laws ran, and took the 'treason songs' with them to sing there. One particular pocket that attracted these courageous incorrigibles was along the Lachlan. Here Ben Hall was born and was killed; and his neighbours and friends enshrined his memory in magnificent home-grown songs.

But before this could happen, the face of the country had been drastically changed by the gold-rush. Not many of the gold-rush songs are anonymous; most of them that survive are the work of professional entertainers, Thatcher, Coxon and others—witty, topical verses set to current overseas hit-tunes for use in the theatres and cabarets of the mushroom gold-towns. They are seldom heard from bush singers today.

Then the alluvial gold petered out. Many towns shrank back into idleness. Unemployment grew serious. Land Acts were passed to alleviate it, but not very successfully. Many squatters were bankrupted by the Land Acts, and went off droving or shearing in the new outback. Others survived as lords of colonial manors, fighting the free-selectors with one hand and the Shearers' Union with the other, piling up 'an overdraft like the National Debt', training cadets of good family in the art of station-management, and encumbering their ornate homesteads with pianos.

Owing to the fact that the cadets (*alias* jackaroos or narangis) were literate we know a fair bit about their singing habits. Living an isolated sort of life midway between the homestead and the men's hut, jackaroos sometimes amused themselves by composing and singing new verses to familiar tunes. Many of the tunes have an air of coming straight from student song books, and some of the verses could be labelled 'school of Adam Lindsay Gordon' without much risk of error.

Now a jackaroo song might find its way to the men's hut, but it would hardly survive there unaltered. The men were professionals, and considered the jackaroos amateurs. They did not share the same vocabulary or the same sense of humour. A song that had been heard from the homestead piano might be amended in the jackaroo barracks, might be re-amended in the hut, and might be passed on to a travelling saddler or an aboriginal droving hand in a condition recalling that of the axe in the proverb: 'It's had two new blades and three new handles, but otherwise it's just as it was when grandfather bought it'.

The men of the nomad trades, the drovers, shearers, bullockies and the rest, were great diffusers of songs; and in addition they composed their own. Drovers were particularly in need of songs to sing as they rode round their beasts at night.

Thus it comes about that the drovers not only borrowed occasional jackaroo-verses at times, but also preserved old bushranging ballads. The shearers too had a healthy taste for the old songs. It was the embattled shearers in the strike of ninety-four who hoisted the Flag of Stars and sang *The Wild Colonial Boy*; and it was an old, old shearer in a Toowoomba hospital who told me: 'That's the way to sing *Bold Jack Donahue*, sonny; not sad, but with a stamp of the foot!'

It was in the late 1880s that the first printing of bush songs occurred, but the first systematic collection was begun by A.B. Paterson in 1898. He published a first thin edition of *The Old Bush Songs* in 1905 and successive enlarged ones until 1932. Many contributors helped him, including the ex-bushranger Jack Bradshaw.

Paterson made another contribution to our folkmusic too, quite distinct from this one. Several of his own poems refused to lie flat on the printed page, but walked off into the bush and grew themselves folktunes. Some of Lawson's did the same.

At the time, Paterson believed that the bush songs were threatened with speedy extinction. The danger seems no more imminent today. The old songs are tough, and die as hard as snakes do. Some types of song which fill a lot of space in his volume are less common now: we hear, for instance, far fewer jackaroo songs than he did. 'Treason songs' on the other hand, still clandestine in 1905, have been more easily collected in recent years. Ballads which he noticed as being sung to overseas tunes have since grown tunes of their own. Some of his texts look unwieldy, as we have become accustomed to versions pruned and compressed by another thirty years of singing. Into the bargain, there is quite a crop of new ballads sprung from the old stock. But the changes are all normal and natural signs of life.

Publication does a doubtful service to folksongs. It preserves them; but it preserves them dead, like stuffed animals in a museum. It brings them to a wide audience; but this includes so many of the wrong people, from school-teachers to hill-billy addicts. The wrong people are those who are bent on taking folksong out of its natural surroundings. Folksong belongs in the home, in the pub, in the foc's'le, in the back of a truck or on a friendly verandah; not in the list of set pieces at an Eisteddfod, not in the schoolroom unless as a rare treat, not between toothpaste advertisements on radio or television. In the alien atmosphere of the concert-hall it takes a great artist to preserve the life and spirit even of his own folksongs, let alone those of other people.

I sometimes wish, in vain, that we could keep up the strict etiquette that was observed by the real bush singers. A young man used to learn his songs from the acknowledged singer of the district, and might eventually earn permission to sing them to the limited 'public' of the bush wherever or whenever the acknowledged singer was not present. Some few songs were common property; others, 'songs from books', were rather contemptuously exempted from the rule; but in the main this apprenticeship system prevailed, at least among men. When the public performer of a 'treason song' might earn a stretch in jail, it was a point of honour to perform it properly.

Today I suppose all songs are 'songs from books', and the songs from this book lose their old status accordingly. It would be nice to think that the demotion might be temporary, and that they might walk off the page back into oral circulation again over a wider stretch of country than the old method could cover.

That this has often been done, can be seen by many of the notes to the individual songs, where I have set out to give the source and background of many oral performances which have led to the inclusion of the songs in this book.

J. S. MANIFOLD

Wynnum, Qld.
1962

1
SEAMEN AND TRANSPORTS

CHANTIES being strictly work-songs, the sailor ashore has little use for them. He is more likely to sing the rowdy forebitters ('off-duty' songs) like 'Maggie May', which are hardly to be distinguished from street-ballads.

Street-ballad ancestry is evident in the convict songs too. The similarity in style between the surviving works of Frank Macnamara, the convict poet, and the surviving convict songs of local origin has led some people to believe that Macnamara wrote these latter as well. I cannot prove or disprove this, but I feel that common descent from Dublin street-balladry would account equally well for the resemblance.

Along with the convict songs which seem to be of local origin, I have included some which originated in the British Isles and were brought out here by later immigrants. It is fairly safe to say that a song which takes a humorous view of convictism arose at some thousands of miles distance from the spot. The nadir of flippant vulgarity is reached with 'Botany Bay', a parody of genuine convict songs, which made the fame and fortune of the London music-hall singer David Belasco James in 1885.

The notes to each song in this part are on page 25 of this book.

BOUND FOR SOUTH AUSTRALIA
(capstan-chanty)

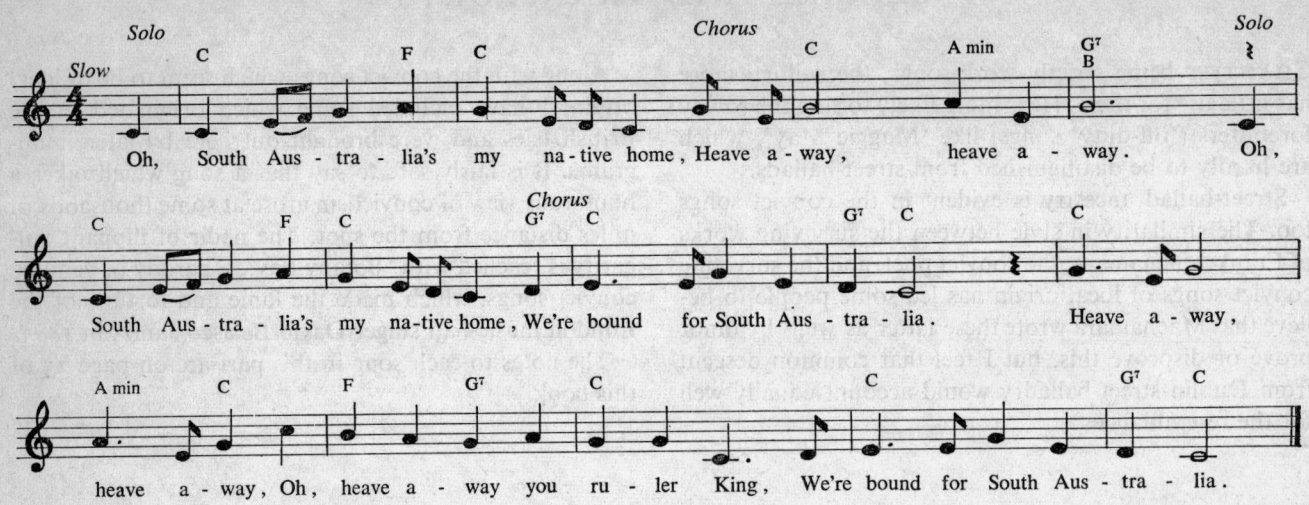

1. SOLO: Oh, South Australia's my native home.
CHORUS: Heave away! Heave away!
SOLO: Oh, South Australia's my native home.
CHORUS: We're bound for South Australia.
        Heave away, heave away,
        Oh heave away, you ruler king,
        We're bound for South Australia.

2. SOLO: There ain't but the one thing grieves my mind.
CHORUS: Heave away! Heave away!
SOLO: To leave my dear wife and child behind.
CHORUS: We're bound for South Australia, *etc.*

(*Solo lines only*)

3.   I see my wife standing on the quay,
       The tears do start as she waves to me.

4.   I'll tell you the truth and I'll tell you no lie;
       If I don't love that girl I hope I may die.

5.   And now I'm bound for a foreign strand,
       With a bottle of whisky in my hand.

6.   I'll drink a glass to the foreign shore,
       And one to the girl that I adore.

THE LITTLE FISH

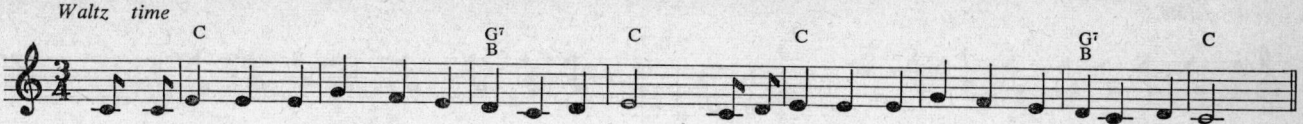

1. There's a song in my heart for the one I love best,
And her picture is tattooed all over my chest.

Chorus: Yea-ho, little fishy, don't cry, don't cry;
Yea-ho, little fishy, don't cry, don't cry.

2. There are fish in the sea, there is no doubt about it,
Just as good as the ones that have ever come out of it.

3. Little fish, when he's caught, he fights like a bull whale,
As he threshes the water with his long narrow tail.

4. The ship's under way and the weather is fine;
The captain's on the bridge hanging out other lines.

5. The crew are asleep, and the ocean's at rest,
And I'm singing this song to the one I love best.

MAGGIE MAY

1. Oh gather round, you sailor boys, and listen to my song,
   And when you've heard it through you'll pity me.
I was a goddam fool in the port of Liverpool
   The first time that I came home from sea.
I was paid off at The Hove from a trip to Sydney Cove –
   And two pound ten a month was all my pay –
Then I started drinking gin, and was neatly taken in
   By a little girl they all called Maggie May.

Chorus: Oh Maggie, Maggie May, they have taken you away
       To slave upon that cold Van Diemen shore!
     For you robbed so many sailors, and dosed so many
                                whalers,
         You'll never cruise down Lime Street any more.

2. 'Twas a damned unlucky day when I first met Maggie May,
   She was cruising up and down old Canning Place;
She had a figure fine as a warship of the line
   And me being a sailor I gave chase.
In the morning when I woke, stiff and sore and stoney broke,
   No trousers, coat or weskit I could find.
The landlady said, 'Sir, I can tell you where they are,
   They'll be down in Stanley's hockshop, number nine.'

3. To the bobby on his beat at the corner of the street,
   To him I went, to him I told my tale.
He asked, as if in doubt: 'Does your mother know you're out?'
   But agreed the lady ought to be in jail.
To the hockshop I applied but no trousers there I spied.
   The bobbies came and took the girl away.
The jury 'guilty' found her, for robbing of a homeward-bounder,
   And paid her passage out to Botany Bay.

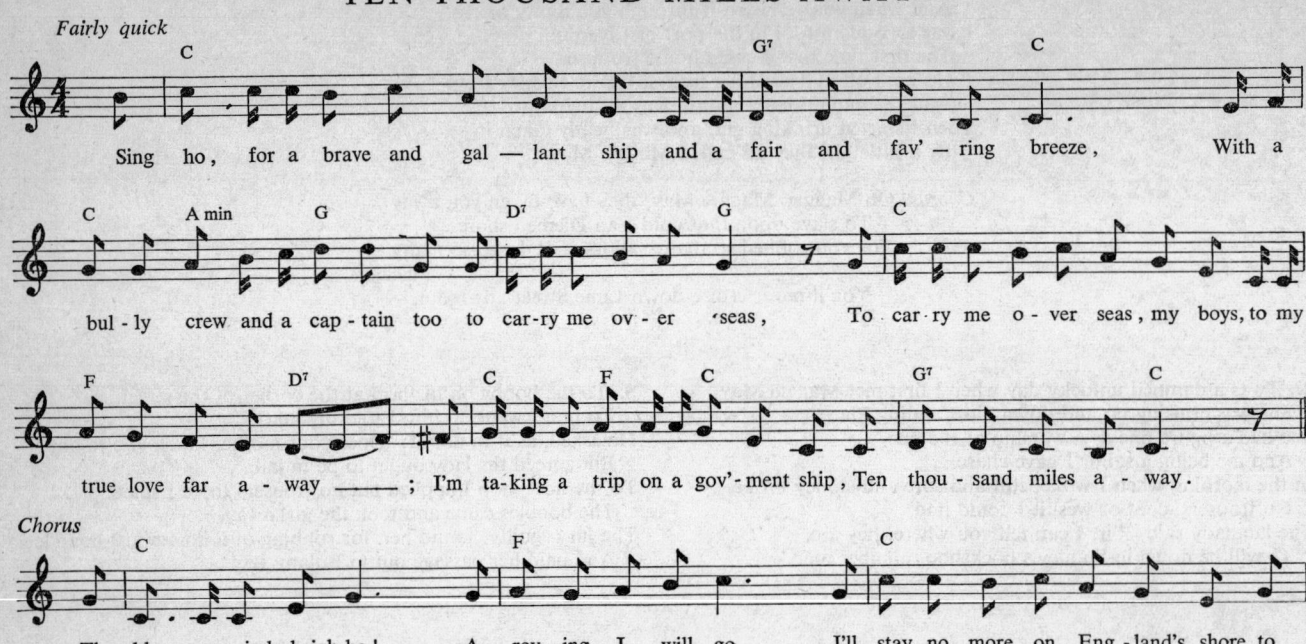

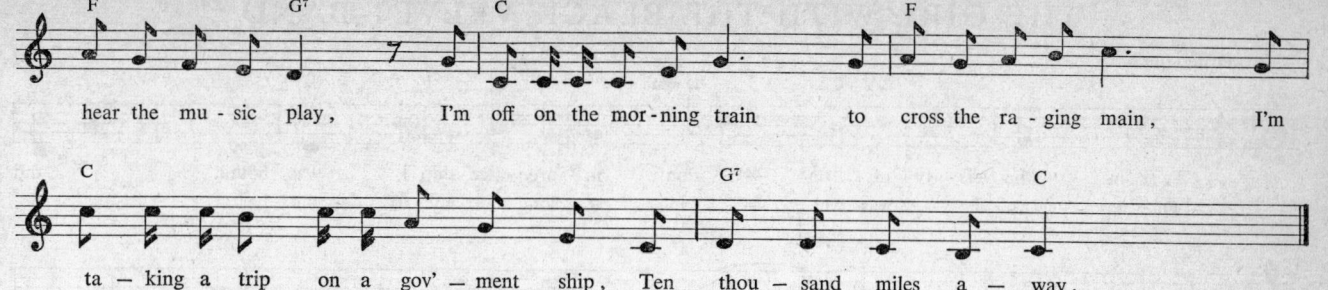

2. My true love she was beautiful,
My true love she was young,
Her eyes were like the diamonds bright,
And silvery was her tongue,
And silvery was her tongue, my boys,
Though she's far away –
She's taken a trip on government ship
Ten thousand miles away.

3. Oh, dark and dismal was the day
When last I seen my Meg;
She'd a government band around each hand,
And another one round her leg;
And another one round her leg, my boys,
As the big ship left the bay –
'Adieu,' said she, 'remember me,
Ten thousand miles away!'

4. I wish I were a bosun bold,
Or even a bombardier,
I'd build a boat and away I'd float,
And straight for my true love steer;
And straight for my true love steer, boys,
Where the dancing dolphins play,
And the whales and the sharks are having their larks
Ten thousand miles away.

5. The sun may shine through a London fog,
Or the river run quite clear;
The ocean's brine be turned to wine,
Or I forget my beer,
Or I forget my beer, my boys,
Or the landlord's quarter day,
Before I forget my own sweetheart
Ten thousand miles away.

THE GIRL WITH THE BLACK VELVET BAND

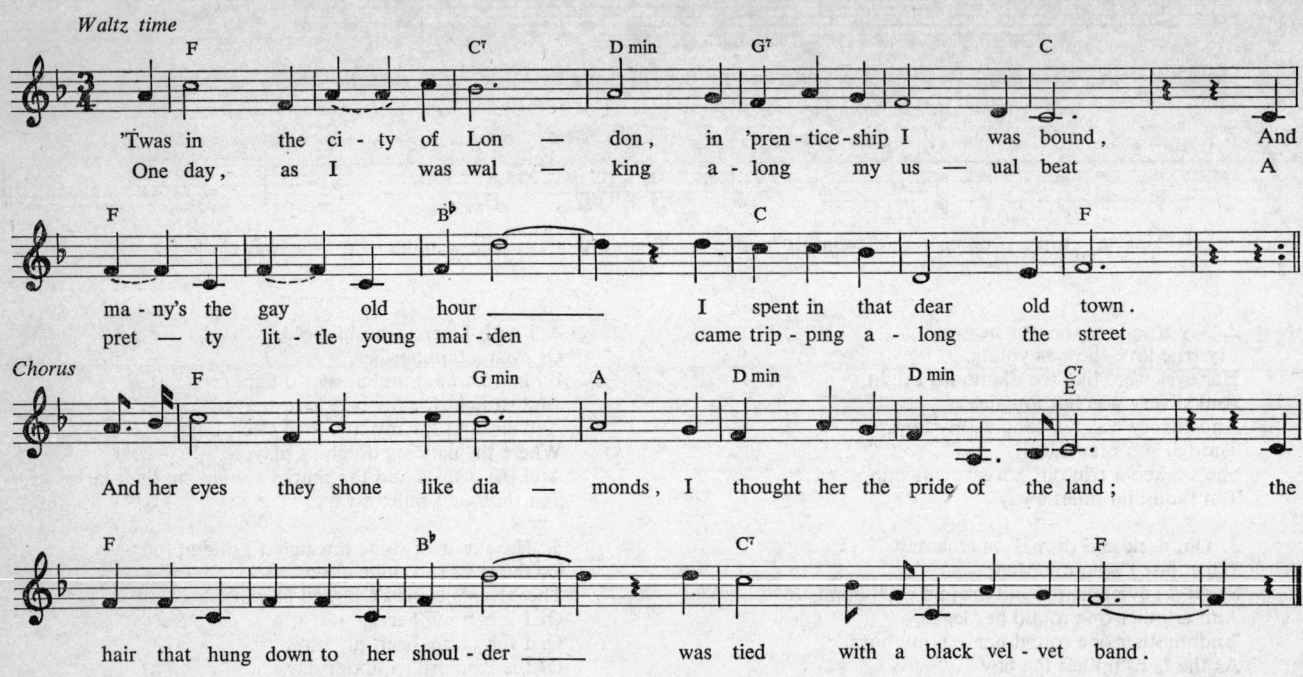

1. 'Twas in the city of London,
In 'prenticeship I was bound
And many's the gay old hour
I spent in that dear old town.
One day as I was walking
Along my usual beat
A pretty little young maiden
Came tripping along the street.

Chorus: And her eyes they shone like diamonds,
I thought her the pride of the land;
The hair that hung down to her shoulder
Was tied with a black velvet band.

2. One day as we were a-walking
A gentleman passed us by;
I could see she was bent on some mischief
By the rolling of her dark blue eye.
Gold watch she picked from his pocket
And slyly placed into my hand;
I was taken in charge by a copper,
Bad luck to that black velvet band.

3. Before the Lord Mayor I was taken,
'Your case, sir, I plainly can see,
And, if I'm not greatly mistaken
You're bound far over the sea.'
It's over the dark and blue ocean,
Far away to Van Diemen's Land,
Away from my friends and relations
And the girl with the black velvet band.

JIM JONES

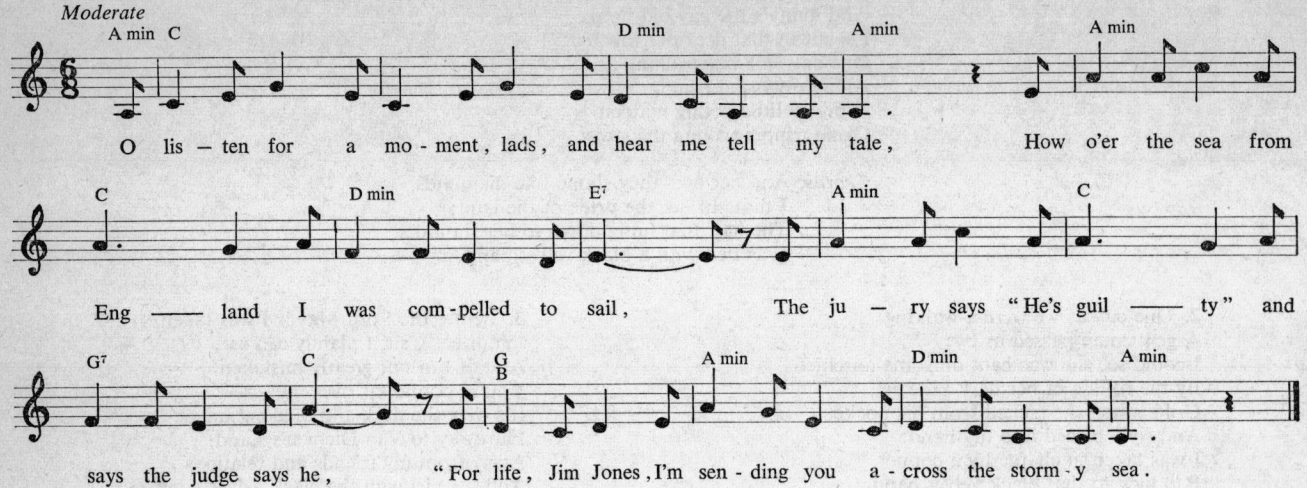

1. O listen for a moment, lads, and hear me tell my tale,
How o'er the sea from England I was compelled to sail.
The jury says 'He's guilty,' and says the judge, says he,
'For life, Jim Jones, I'm sending you across the stormy sea.

2. 'And take my tip before you ship to join the iron gang;
Don't get too gay at Botany Bay, or else you'll surely hang –
Or else you'll hang,' he says, says he, 'and after that, Jim Jones,
High up upon the gallows tree the crows will pick your bones.

3. 'You'll have no time for mischief then, remember what I say;
They'll flog the poaching out of you, out there at Botany Bay.'
The waves were high upon the sea, the winds blew up in gales –
I would rather drown in misery than go to New South Wales.

4. The winds blew high upon the sea, and the pirates came along,
But the soldiers on our convict ship were full five hundred strong.
They opened fire and somehow drove that pirate ship away,
I'd rather have joined that pirate ship than come to Botany Bay.

5. For day and night the irons clang, and like poor galley-slaves
We toil and toil, and when we die must fill dishonoured graves.
But by and by I'll break my chain; into the bush I'll go,
And join the brave bushrangers there, Jack Donahue & Co.

6. And some dark night when everything is silent in the town
I'll kill the tyrants one and all, I'll shoot the floggers down;
I'll give the Law a little shock, remember what I say:
They'll yet regret they sent Jim Jones in chains to Botany Bay.

VAN DIEMEN'S LAND

1. Come all you gallant poaching boys that ramble free of care,
That rove out on a moonlit night with gun and dog and snare.
The hare and lofty pheasant you have at your command,
Never thinking of your last career upon Van Diemen's Land.

2. Poor Tommy Brown from Nenagh Town, Jack Murphy and poor Joe,
We was three daring poachers as the gentry well do know.
One night we were trepanned by the keepers hid in the sand,
Who for fourteen years transported us into Van Diemen's Land.

3. The first day that we landed here upon the fatal shore,
The settlers came around us, some twenty score or more;
They ranked us up like horses and they sold us out of hand,
And they yoked us up to ploughing-frames to plough Van Diemen's Land.

4. The hovels that we're living in are built of mud and clay,
With rotten straw for bedding, and to that we daren't say nay.
They fence us in with raging fire, and we slumber as we can,
But it keeps away the wolves and tigers upon Van Diemen's Land.

5. There was a girl from Newport, Susan Somers was her name,
And she had been transported for playing of the game;
But she took the captain's fancy and he married her out of hand,
And she gives us all good treatment upon Van Diemen's Land.

6. It's often when in slumber I have had a pleasant dream;
With my sweetheart I've been sitting down beside a crystal stream;
Through Ireland I've gone roaming with my sweetheart by the hand;
Then I wake up broken-hearted upon Van Diemen's Land.

7. So all you lively poaching lads, this warning take from me:
I'd have you quit night walking and avoid bad company,
And throw aside your guns and snares, for let me tell you plain;
If you knew of our misfortunes you would never poach again.

MORETON BAY

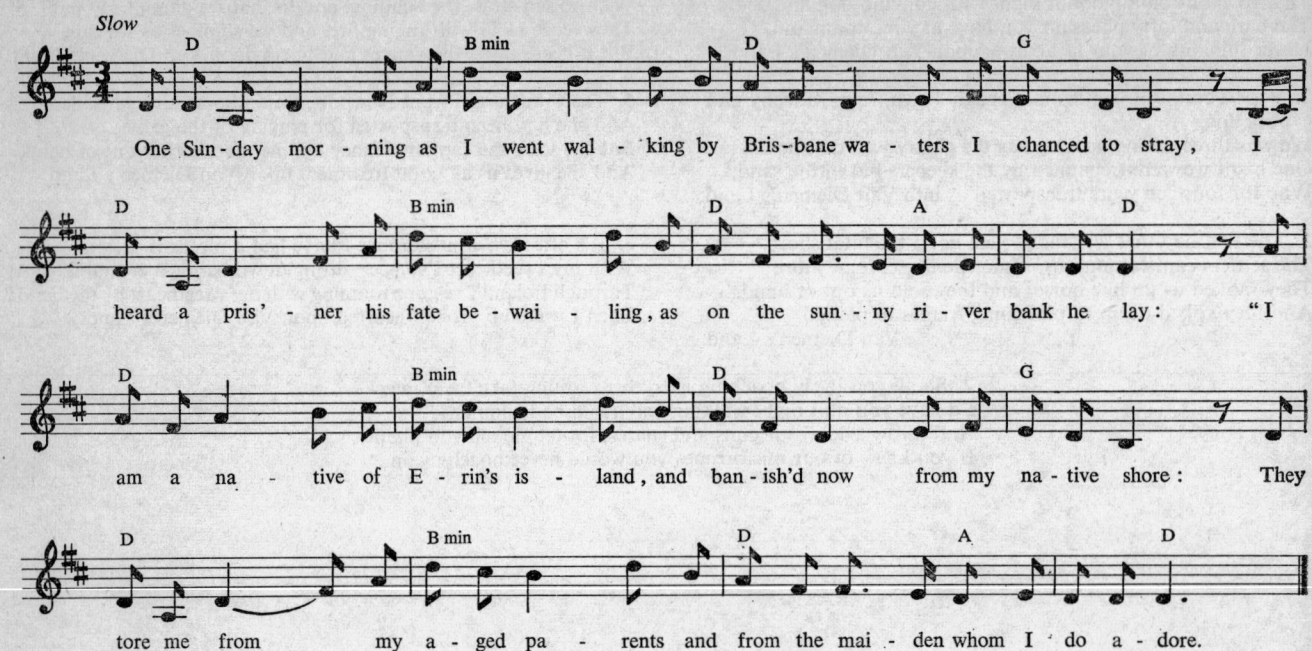

MORETON BAY
(another tune)

1. One Sunday morning as I went walking, by Brisbane waters I chanced to stray;
I heard a prisoner his fate bewailing, as on the sunny river bank he lay:
'I am a native of Erin's island and banished now from my native shore;
They tore me from my aged parents and from the maiden whom I do adore.

2. 'I've been a prisoner at Port Macquarie, at Norfolk Island and Emu Plains,
At Castle Hill and at cursed Toongabbie, at all those settlements I've worked in chains;
But of all places of condemnation and penal stations of New South Wales,
To Moreton Bay I have found no equal; excessive tyranny each day prevails.

3. 'For three long years I was beastly treated, and heavy irons on my legs I wore;
My back with flogging is lacerated and often painted with my crimson gore.
And many a man from downright starvation lies mouldering now underneath the clay;
And Captain Logan he had us mangled at the triangles of Moreton Bay.

4. 'Like the Egyptians and ancient Hebrews we were oppressed under Logan's yoke,
Till a native black lying there in ambush did give our tyrant his mortal stroke,
My fellow prisoners, be exhilarated that all such monsters such a death may find!
And when from bondage we are liberated our former sufferings shall fade from mind.'

THE CONVICT MAID

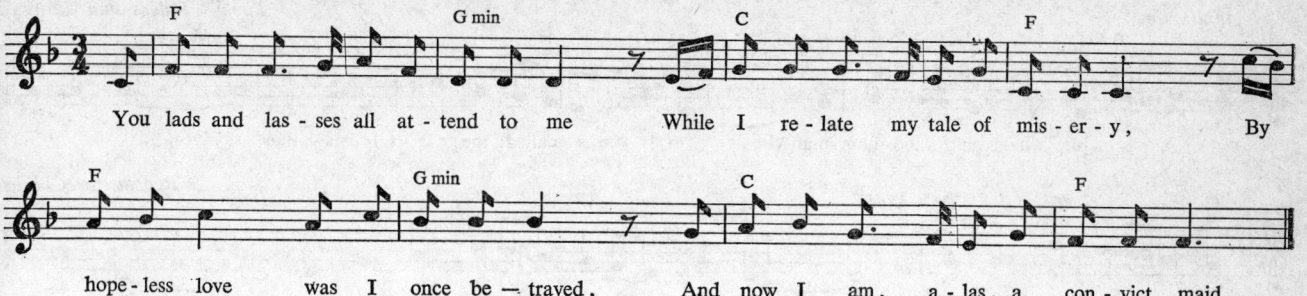

1. You lads and lasses all attend to me
While I relate my tale of misery;
By hopeless love was I once betrayed,
And now I am, alas, a Convict Maid.

2. To please my lover did I try so sore,
That I spent upon him all my master's store,
Who in his wrath did so loud upbraid
And brought before the judge this Convict Maid.

3. The judge his sentence then to me addressed
Which filled with agony my aching breast:
'To Botany Bay you must be conveyed
For seven long years to be a Convict Maid.'

4. For seven long years I toil in pain and grief,
And curse the day that I became a thief.
Oh had I stuck by some honest trade,
I ne'er had been, alas, a Convict Maid.

THE CATALPA

1. A noble whale ship and commander,
Was called the Catalpa, they say,
She came out to Western Australia
And took six poor Fenians away.

Chorus: So come all you screw warders and jailers,
Remember Perth regatta day,
Take care of the rest of your Fenians,
Or the Yankees will steal them away.

2. Seven long years had they served here
And seven long more had to stay,
For defending their own country, Old Ireland,
For that they were banished away.

3. You kept them in Western Australia
Till their hair began to turn grey,
When a Yank from the States of America
Came out here and stole them away.

4. Now all the Perth boats were a-racing,
And making short tacks for the spot;
But the Yankee she tacked into Fremantle,
And took the best prize of the lot.

5. The Georgette, armed with bold warriors,
Went out the poor Yanks to arrest,
But she hoisted her star-spangled banner,
Saying, 'You'll not board me, I guess.'

6. So remember those six Fenians colonial
And sing o'er these few verses with skill,
And remember the Yankee that stole them
And the home that they left on the hill.

7. Now they've landed safe in America
And there will be able to cry,
'Hoist up the green flag and shamrock,
Hurrah for old Ireland we'll die.'

BOTANY BAY

Repeat for Chorus

1. Farewell to old England for ever,
Farewell to my rum culls as well;
Farewell to the well-known old Bailee,
Where I used for to cut such a swell.

Chorus: Singing too-ral li-ooral li-ad-dity
Singing too-ral li-ooral li-ay;
Singing too-ral li-ooral li-ad-dity
Singing too-ral li-ooral li-ay.

2. There's the Captain as is our Commander,
There's the bo'sun and all the ship's crew,
There's the first and second-class passengers,
Knows what we poor convicts go through.

3. 'Taint leavin' old England we cares about,
'Taint cos we mispels what we knows,
But becos all we light-fingered gentry
Hops around with a log on our toes.

4. For seven long years I'll be staying here,
For seven long years and a day,
For meeting a cove in an area
And taking his ticker away.

5. Oh, had I the wings of a turtle-dove!
I'd soar on my pinions so high,
Slap bang to the arms of my Polly love,
And in her sweet presence I'd die.

6. Now, all my young Dookies and Duchesses,
Take warning from what I've to say,
Mind all is your own as you touchesses,
Or you'll find us in Botany Bay.

MY LAST FAREWELL TO STIRLING

1. Nae lark in transport mounts the sky
Nor leaves with early plaintive cry,
But I maun bid my last goodbye,
   My last farewell to Stirling-O.

2. Nae mair I'll wander through the glen
To rob the roost o' the pheasant hen,
Nor chase the rabbits to their den
   When I am far frae Stirling-O.

3. Now fare ye weel, my dearest dear,
For you I'll shed a bitter tear,
But may you find some other dear
   When I am far frae Stirling-O.

4. Now fare ye weel, for I am bound
For twenty years to Van Diemen's Land,
But speak of me and of what I've done
   When I am far frae Stirling-O.

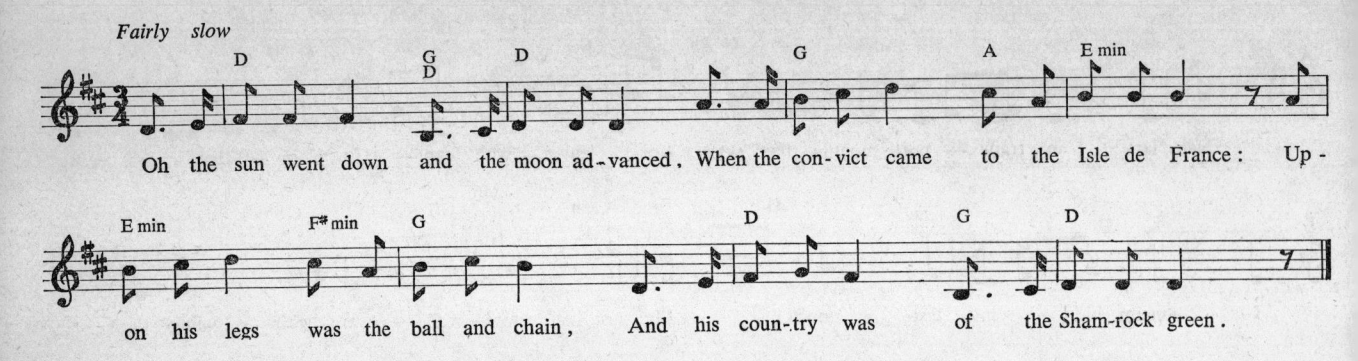

THE ISLE DE FRANCE

Fairly slow

Oh the sun went down and the moon ad-vanced, When the con-vict came to the Isle de France: Upon his legs was the ball and chain, And his coun-try was of the Sham-rock green.

1. Oh, the sun went down, and the moon advanced
   When the convict came to the Isle de France;
   Upon his leg was the ring and chain,
   And his country was of the Shamrock green.

2. Then the coastguard came to the island beach
   Till the convict's boat was within the reach,
   And he asked, while tears from his eyes did rain,
   'Were you born, young man, of the Shamrock green?'

3. 'Oh I am a Shamrock', the convict cried,
   'That has been tossed on the ocean wide!
   'For being unruly, I do declare,
   'I was doomed a transport for seven years.

4. 'When six of these was past and gone,
'We were coming home for to make up one,
'When the stormy winds did so blow and roar
'I was cast up here on this foreign shore'.

5. Then a speedy letter went to the Queen
About the shipwreck of the Shamrock green,
Then his freedom came by a speedy post
To the absent convict they thought was lost.

6. 'God bless the coastguard!' the convict cried,
'Who saved my life from the ocean wide.
'I will drink his health in a flowing glass,
'So here's success to the Isle de France!'

NOTES

BOUND FOR SOUTH AUSTRALIA

The capstan-chanty version was collected by Ron Edwards in Victoria, and published in *Bandicoot Ballads*. The accentuation of various lines has been altered here in the light of other versions collected since. I am told that the crew of S.S. *Flinders* 'sang the old tub to rest' with this beautiful tune, on her last voyage in 1923 to the shipbreakers. The halyard-chanty was collected in 1956 by the Queensland Folklore Society. Slight variant tune *Singabout*, Vol. 1, No. 1.

THE LITTLE FISH

A foc'sle song from the Queensland coast. A composite from versions printed in *Singabout*, Vol. 2, No. 4, and Vol. 3, No. 2. I have fitted the supplementary verses in at what seemed to me to be the best places, but claim no authenticity for this order. The original sources were Dick Fitzgerald of Charleville, and Jack Wright of Coogee.

MAGGIE MAY

A foc'sle song of Liverpool origin apparently, but immensely popular among seamen all over the world. This version comes chiefly from Geoff Wills, late of S.S. *Cycle*, with amendments and interpolations from the version published in *Singabout*, Vol. 2, No. 2, from 'Scouse' at the Raby Bay hotel, South Queensland, from Alec Lewis and others.

TEN THOUSAND MILES AWAY

This is just as international as 'Maggie May' but became even more widely known in Australia, where it provided a tune and a formula for several later ballads. This version was collected by Dr Russel Ward, of New England University. The *Scottish Students' Songbook* attributes the original to J.F. Geogehan. There are some excellent variant verses, notably about the lady who had:

> Golden hair right down to *there*
> And a sweet deluding tongue.

The tune is close to that of the 'Old Palmer Song' and 'Hurrah for Roma Railway'. (*Queensland Pocket Songbook*).

THE GIRL WITH THE BLACK VELVET BAND

Highly popular in the outback in the 1880s according to Keighley Goodchild. This version and others were collected by John Meredith and published in *The Canon*, January 1959.

JIM JONES

The words were collected and written down by the late Charles MacAlister of Currabungla in his *Old Pioneering Days*. This slightly fuller version was collected by John Meredith. The tune was said to be 'Irish Molly-O', but it is not the 'Irish Molly-O' that I used to hear in Antrim in 1943-4.

VAN DIEMEN'S LAND

One of the oldest and the most widespread of our songs. My impression is that it spread from Tasmania in goldrush times, both to the mainland and back to the British Isles. Tom Collins knew it when he was a young man (see *The Buln-Buln and the Brolga*) in Victoria. It has been reported from as far North as Rockhampton, Queensland, as well as from Ireland, Scotland, and the English Midlands. This version, substantially that of *Bandicoot Ballads*, is the one I learnt first, long before the war, and have been modifying according to the hints of other singers ever since. The 'Susan' verse was given to me quite recently in Brisbane. 'Playing of the game' appears to mean prostitution: compare seventeenth-century English and nineteenth-century American usage of the word 'sport'.

MORETON BAY

A ballad with a long unwritten history. Captain Logan was speared in October 1830. Ned Kelly quotes lines from the ballad in his *Jerilderie Letter* (1879). Jack Bradshaw, self-styled 'last of the bushrangers', wrote down a very full version in or before 1911, in his *True History* and appears to associate it with Kelly. Later Bradshaw reprinted it in *Twenty Years of Prison Life*, subtitling it: 'On Poor Old Frank McNamara'. In 1916, J.R. Scott obtained a manuscript in Queensland which is startingly true to Bradshaw's. In 1944, Will Lawson printed the Scott MS in *Australian Bush Songs and Ballads*. In 1952 with the help of Warren Bowden and Bill Scott, I assembled the *Bandicoot Ballads* text here reprinted, using their pooled recollections and a few essential lines from the Bradshaw text. This is a singer's text. The original reads more like a recitation. The alternative was recorded by the Folklore Society of Victoria from the singing of Mr Simon McDonald of Creswick, who learnt it from his uncle, Jack McDonald, born in 1850, a ganger on the Victorian Railways.

Mr McDonald's verses differ from those printed on page 18. His first verse runs:

> I am a native of the land of Erin;
>   I was early banished from my native shore,
> On the ship *Columbus* when circular sailing,
>   And I left behind me the girl I adore.
> O'er the bounding billows which were loudly raging,
>   Like a bold sea-mariner my course did steer.
> We were bound for Sydney, our destination,
>   And every day in irons wore.

Then follows a kind of refrain similar to the second of the verses published with the tune:

> Oh Moreton Bay, you'll find no equal,
>   Norfolk Island and Emu Plains;
> At Castle Hill and cursed Toongabbie,
>   And old-time places in New South Wales.

His second verse includes these lines:

> When I arrived, 'twas in Port Jackson,
>   And I thought my days would happy be.
> But I found out I was greatly mistaken,
>   I was taken a prisoner to Moreton Bay;

plus the first half of our third verse. His third verse is our fourth verse; and he repeats his 'refrain' after that.

THE CATALPA

Collected by Dr Russel Ward from V. Courtney, Perth. I heard the chorus, tacked on to different and satirical words, during World

War 2 from 18 Brigade troops. Edgar Waters, of the Australian National University, Canberra, supplied me with the English original of the tune 'Judges and Juries', just in time to prevent me in my ignorance mistaking it from an out-of-tune 'Botany Bay'.

BOTANY BAY

Not to be mistaken for a 'dinkum' convict song. This is evidently a theatrical parody of the genuine thing, such as the 'Judges and Juries' mentioned above, and probably by way of the street-ballad version printed by Hugh Anderson in *Colonial Ballads* (F.W. Cheshire, Melbourne, 1960; second edition). It was introduced into the musical-comedy *Little Jack Shepherd* (London 1885, Melbourne 1886) and sung with immense success by the comedian David Belasco James.

MY LAST FAREWELL TO STIRLING

I heard the tune and a few of the words on the Darling Downs in 1954, but have mislaid my journal of this trip, so regretfully cannot give a precise source. The remaining verses are supplied from Ewan McColl's collection, *Scotland Sings*.

THE ISLE DE FRANCE

The tune and first verse were sung to me in March 1962 by Mrs Webb, now of Toowong, who learnt the song as a girl on the south coast of N.S.W. In May 1964 Mr Hugh Anderson of Melbourne showed me a broadsheet version, very long and without tune, from which I have extracted the other verses given here.

The Isle de France was ceded to Britain in 1814 and was later renamed Mauritius. The ballad appears to date from before the change of name, yet the 'letter to the Queen' hints at after 1837.

THE CONVICT MAID

This is evidently of street-ballad origin. Geoffrey Ingleton prints a very similar ballad in *True Patriots All*. This version is from *The Queensland Pocket Songbook*.

2
IMMIGRANTS AND DIGGERS

The new-chum has always been a comic figure. The free immigrant of the earlies, unless he was 'gentry' and hated, was the despised butt of the convict old-hands. What are grouped here as immigrant songs are more often *about* immigrants than *by* immigrants, and they represent a type of song distinct from the convict-songs; a tolerated and rather superficial entertainment.

In the fifties, the new-chum digger replaced the old-style immigrant as a butt. On the goldfields, however, the diggers developed their own *esprit de corps*, and made pets of the professional entertainers who romanticised their life. The songs given here include a few by known authors which have passed into oral circulation.

There is a disappointing lack of songs about Eureka Stockade. I imagine that the professional entertainers were too much under the eye of the police to mention the subject, and the growth of anonymous songs would be checked by the impermanence and transience of digger population.

The notes to each song in this part are on page 44 of this book.

THE POMMY'S LAMENT

Moderate

All you on e-mi-gra-tion bent, with home and Eng-land dis-con-tent, Come lis-ten to my sad la-ment a-bout the bush of Aus-tra-lia.

Chorus

Il-la-war-ra, Mit-ta-gong, Par-ra-mat-ta, Wol-lon-gong, If you wish to be-come an or-ang-ou-tang, Well go to the bush of Aus-tra-lia.

1. All you on emigration bent,
With home and England discontent,
Come listen to my sad lament
About the bush of Australia.

Chorus: Illawarra, Mittagong,
Parramatta, Wollongong,
If you wish to become an orang-outang
Well, go to the bush of Australia.

2. Once I possessed a thousand pounds,
Says I to meself how grand it sounds,
For a man to be farming his own grounds
In the promising land of Australia.

3. When coming out the ship got lost,
In a very sad plight we reached the coast,
And very nearly made a roast
For the savages of Australia.

4. Escaped from thence I lighted on
A fierce bushranger with his gun,
Who borrowed my garments, every one,
For himself in the bush of Australia.

5. Sydney town we reached at last,
Says I to meself, all danger's passed,
Now I'll make me fortune fast
In the promising land of Australia.

6. So off I went with cash in hand,
Upon the map I bought the land,
But found it nought but barren sand
When I got to the bush of Australia.

7. Of sheep I got a famous lot;
Some died of hunger, some of rot,
But the divil a lot of rain we got
In this promising land of Australia.

8. My convicts, they were always drunk,
And kept me in a mighty funk,
Says I to meself as to bed I sunk,
I wish I were out of Australia.

9. Of ills I've had enough, you'll own,
But something else my woes to crown,
One night my bark hut tumbled down,
And settled me in Australia.

10. Of cash and homestead thus bereft,
The ruddy spot I gladly left,
Making it over by deed of gift
To the savages of Australia.

11. Now stones upon the road I break,
And earn my seven bob a week,
'Tis better surely than the freak
Of settling down in Australia.

SIXTEEN THOUSAND MILES FROM HOME

Oh I'm six-teen thou-sand miles from home, and me heart is fair-ly a-ching, To think that I should hum-ble so to come out here stone-break-ing, The road I took was Bung-re-oo an' I met with a sub-con-trac—tor, Who eyed me and stud-ied me as a par-son or a doc—tor, With me hoo-ral, doo-ral tid-dy-fal-oo-ral tid-dy-fal-oll-de-i-doh.

1. Oh, I'm sixteen thousand miles from home
   An' me heart is fairly achin',
To think that I should humble so
   To come out here stone breakin'.
The road I took was Bungreoo
   An' I met with a sub-contractor,
Who eyed me an' studied me
   As a parson or a doctor.

Chorus: With me hooral dooral,
          Tiddy falooral,
          Tiddy faloll dee-i-doh.

2. Now I told him I was out of work,
   An' wanted some employment.
He sez 'You do! You stink with scent,
   You've had too much enjoyment.
Go over on to yonder hill,
   Get from the boss a hammer,
An' nine an' six it is your pay,
   An' mind you now, that's grammar.'
With me hooral dooral, *etc.*

3. So I battered and whacked the whole of the day,
   At evening I grew spiteful;
With the sight I didn't know what to do,
   I hadn't broke me hatful.
Just then the boss he came along,
   Sez he, 'You'll have to alter,
You'll be gettin' no run o' the store, be Gosh,
   You'll never make your salt, sir.'
With me hooral dooral, *etc.*

4. So I chucked me hammer down on the heap,
   With that I did consider,
I knocked the dust from off me boots,
   An' battered me old black beaver,
Bad luck then to the mam an' dad,
   That reared me up so lazy,
With a silver spoon I'm a regular loon,
   With hunger I'm very near crazy.
With me hooral dooral, *etc.*

5. Now I'll go and list the army,
   I'll go and list the rifle,
An' if I get shot I'll forget the lot,
   All pastime an' all trifle.
With me hooral dooral, *etc.*

BILLY BARLOW IN AUSTRALIA

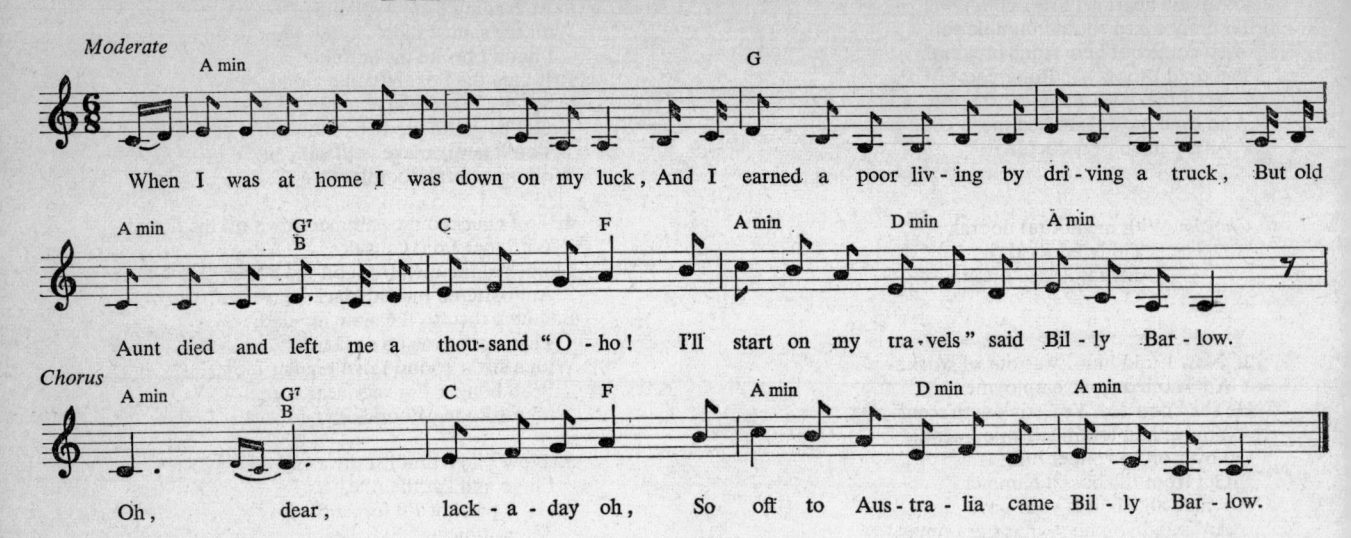

Moderate

When I was at home I was down on my luck, And I earned a poor liv-ing by dri-ving a truck, But old Aunt died and left me a thou-sand "O-ho! I'll start on my tra-vels" said Bil-ly Bar-low.

Chorus

Oh, dear, lack-a-day oh, So off to Aus-tra-lia came Bil-ly Bar-low.

34

1. When I was at home I was down on my luck,
And I earned a poor living by driving a truck;
But old aunt died, and left me a thousand – 'Oho!
I'll start on my travels,' said Billy Barlow.

Chorus: Oh dear, lackaday, oh,
    So off to Australia came Billy Barlow.

2. When to Sydney I got, there a merchant I met,
Who said he would teach me a fortune to get;
He had cattle and sheep past the colony's bounds,
Which he sold with the station for my thousand pounds.
Oh dear, lackaday, oh,
He gammoned the cash out of Billy Barlow.

3. So I got my supplies and I gave him my bill,
And for New England started, my pockets to fill;
But by bushrangers met, with my traps they made free,
Took my horse and left Billy tied up to a tree.
Oh dear, lackaday, oh,
'I shall die of starvation,' thought Billy Barlow.

4. At last I got loose, and I then did repair
For my station once more, and at length I got there;
But a few days before that, the blacks, you must know,
Had speared all the cattle of Billy Barlow.
Oh dear, lackaday, oh,
'It's a beautiful country,' says Billy Barlow.

5. And for nine months before, no rain there had been,
So the devil a blade of grass was to be seen;
One third of my wethers the scab they had got,
And the other two-thirds had just died of the rot.
Oh dear, lackaday, oh,
'I shall soon be a settler,' said Billy Barlow.

. . .

6. I'm in Sydney, insolvent, in poverty's toil;
I've no cattle for salting, no sheep for to boil;
I can't get a job – though to any I'd stoop,
If 'twas only the making of portable soup.
Oh dear, lackaday, oh,
Pray give some employment to Billy Barlow.

WITH MY SWAG ALL ON MY SHOULDER
(*or* Denis O'Riley)

March time

When first I left old Ireland's shore, the yarns that we were told Of how the folks in far Aus-tra — li-a could pick up lumps of gold! How gold-dust lay in all the streets and miner's right was free! "Hur-rah!" I told my lov-ing friends "That's just the place for me!" *repeat for Chorus*

With my swag all on my shoul—der, black bil-ly in my hand I'll travel the bushes of Aus-tra—li-a like a true born I—rish man.

1. When first I left Old Ireland's shore, the yarns that we were told
Of how the folks in far Australia could pick up lumps of gold!
How gold-dust lay in all the streets and miner's right was free!
'Hurrah!' I told my loving friends, 'That's just the place for me.'

Chorus: With my swag all on my shoulder, black billy in my hand,
I'll travel the bushes of Australia like a trueborn Irishman.

2. When first we reached Port Melbourne we were all prepared to slip,
And bar the captain and the mate all hands abandoned ship.
And all the girls of Melbourne town threw up their arms with joy,
Hurrooing and exclaiming, 'Here comes my Irish boy!'

Chorus: With his swag all on his shoulder, black billy in his hand,
He'll travel the bushes of Australia like a trueborn Irishman.

3. We made our way into Geelong, then north to Ballarat,
Where some of us grew mighty thin, and some grew sleek and fat.
Some tried their luck at Bendigo and some at Fiery Creek;
I made my fortune in a day and blued it in a week!

Chorus: With my swag all on my shoulder, black billy in my hand,
I travelled the bushes of Australia like a trueborn Irishman.

4. For many years I wandered round to each new field about,
And made and spent full many a pound till alluvial petered out.
And then for any job of work I was prepared to try,
But now I've found the tucker track, I'll stay there till I die.

Chorus: With my swag all on my shoulder, black billy in my hand,
I'll travel the bushes of Australia like a trueborn Irishman.

THE OLD PALMER SONG

The wind is fair and free, my boys, the wind is fair and free. The steamer's course is north, my boys, and the Palmer we will see. The Palmer we will see, my boys, and Cooktown's muddy shore Where I've been told there's lots of gold, so stay down south no more.

repeat for Chorus

1. The wind is fair and free, my boys,
The wind is fair and free;
The steamer's course is north, my boys,
And the Palmer we will see.
And the Palmer we will see, my boys,
And Cooktown's muddy shore,
Where I've been told there's lots of gold
So stay down South no more.

Chorus: So, blow ye winds, heigho!
A digging we will go,
I'll stay no more down South, my boys,
So let the music play.
In spite of what I'm told,
I'm off to search for gold,
And make a push for that new rush
A thousand miles away.

2. I hear the blacks are troublesome,
And spear both horse and man,
The rivers all are wide and deep,
No bridges them do span.
No bridges them do span, my boys,
And so you'll have to swim,
But never fear the yarns you hear
And gold you're sure to win.

3. So let us make a move, my boys,
For that new promised land,
And do the best we can, my boys,
To lend a helping hand.
To lend a helping hand, my boys,
Where the soil is rich and new;
In spite of blacks and unknown tracks,
We'll show what we can do.

TAMBAROORA GOLD

Version I

It was just about a year ago as near as I can guess When I left dear old Sydney Town in trouble and distress.

Version II

My friends and sweetheart slighted me and gave me turnips cold, Until a voice cried in my ear "Try Tambaroora gold!"

1. It was just about a year ago, as near as I can guess,
When I left dear old Sydney Town in trouble and distress.
My friends and sweetheart slighted me and gave me turnips cold,
Until a voice cried in my ear, 'Try Tambaroora gold!'

2. The day I left old Sydney Town, a tear fell from my eye;
Of all my friends there was not one to say to me goodbye.
So I wandered on my journey, and quite soon I did behold
The hills that glittered brightly with bright Tambaroora gold.

3. I'd not been long upon the fields before I got a job
And worked six months for wages with a chap named Dusty Bob.
With that a claim I purchased, and while turning up the mould,
My pile I soon created with bright Tambaroora gold.

4. Then I came back to Sydney Town, a regular dashing swell,
And strange to say my previous friends all seemed to wish me well.
They lowly bowed and touched their hats as up the street I strolled;
But, thinks I, they don't want Johnny but his Tambaroora gold.

5. When I walked down the street last night, by someone I was told
To stand and to deliver up my Tambaroora gold.
I flew into him madly; in the gutter as we rolled
He cried, 'Spare my days, and Devil take your Tambaroora gold.'

6. The other day as I strolled out I met Eileen Arvone,
Who once gave me cold turnips when she found my money gone.
Said she, 'Come to my bosom, John, we'll be lovers as of old.'
But says I, 'You don't love Johnny but his Tambaroora gold.'

    7. (So all you bold young diggers, attend to my advice,
    And don't trust man or woman till you've looked them over twice)
    I have travelled for experience and have many a time been sold,
    But this time they won't get Johnny or his Tambaroora gold.

LOOK OUT BELOW!

1. A young man left his native town,
Through trade being slack at home,
To seek his fortune in this land
He crossed the briny foam.

2. And when he came to the Lachlan,
His heart was in a glow,
To hear the sound of the windlasses,
And the cry 'Look out below!'

3. Where'er he turned his wondering eyes,
Strange sights he did behold
Of full and plenty in the land
And the magic power of gold.

4. He says: 'Now I am young and strong,
And a-digging I will go,
For I like the sound of the windlasses,
And the cry "Look out below!"'

5. So now he's settled down again
With a charming little wife,
He says there's nothing can come up
To a jolly digger's life.

6. Ask him if he'll go home again
And he'll quickly answer 'No,'
For he likes the sound of the windlasses
And the cry 'Look out below!'

THE MINER

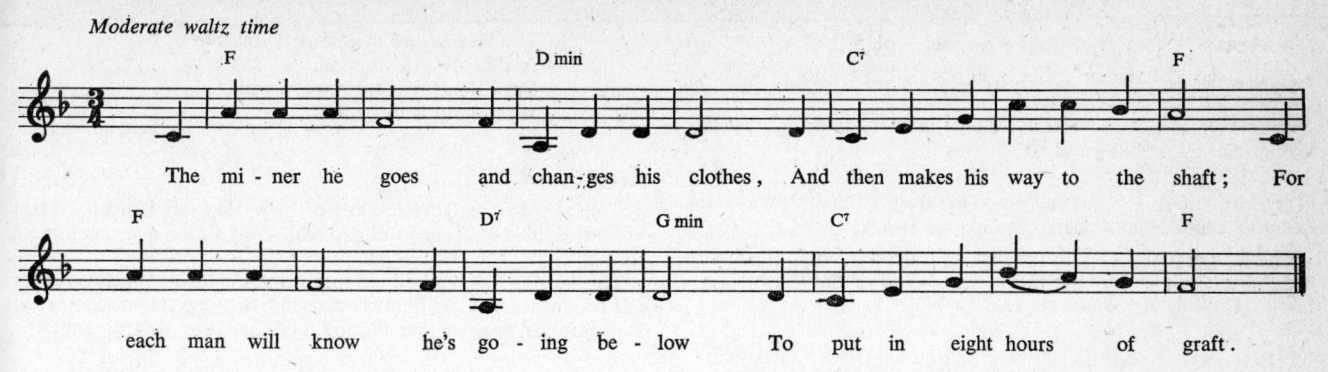

1. The miner he goes and changes his clothes,
   And then makes his way to the shaft;
For each man will know he's going below
   To put in eight hours of graft.

Chorus: With his calico cap and his old flannel shirt,
   His pants with the strap round the knee,
   His boots watertight and his candle alight,
   His crib and his billy of tea.

2. The tapman to the driver will knock four and one,
   The ropes to the windlass will strain;
As one shift comes up, another goes down,
   And working commences again.

3. He works hard for his pay at six bob a day,
   He toils for his missus and kids.
He gets what's left over, and thinks he's in clover
   To cut off his baccy from quids.

4. And thus he goes on, week in and week out,
   To toil for his life's daily bread.
He's off to the mine in hail, rain or shine,
   That his dear ones at home may be fed.

5. Digging holes in the ground where there's gold to be found,
   (And most times where gold it is not)
A man's like a rabbit with this digging habit,
   And like one he ought to be shot.

NOTES

THE POMMY'S LAMENT, from *Singabout*, Vol. 3, No. 3.

Also given in Paterson's *Old Bush Songs*, but without the tune.

SIXTEEN THOUSAND MILES FROM HOME, from *Singabout*, Vol. 3, No. 2 – spelling and all!

BILLY BARLOW IN AUSTRALIA. Text from Paterson's *Old Bush Songs* and tune from Anderson's *Colonial Ballads*.

This was actually sung to me first, to a different tune (probably not folktune either), by the Bush Music Club of the Presbyterian Ladies' College, Armidale, New South Wales.

WITH MY SWAG ALL ON MY SHOULDER (*or* Denis O'Riley)

Given as two different songs in Stewart and Keesing, *Old Bush Songs*, but sung in this form by Father P.P. Kehoe of Kyabram, Victoria, who also uses the fine Irish tune given here. The tune published in *Speewah* is similar but less ornamental.

THE OLD PALMER SONG. Words are from *The Native Companion Songster*.

The tune is as printed in Section 1 of this volume, 'Ten Thousand Miles Away'. There is a variant verse 2, sung by Doug Eaton and others, as follows:

> They say the blacks make fierce attacks,
> On horse and man up there;
> They say the creeks are in flood for weeks
> And bridges are mighty rare.
> The bridges are mighty rare, my boys,
> And crocodiles abound,
> But I don't fear the yarns I hear
> When gold is to be found.

TAMBAROORA GOLD

Collected by Dr Russel Ward of New England University and published in *Singabout*, Vol. 4, No. 3, in fuller but incomplete form.

This version has been edited into printable form. *Singabout* gives two fragmentary tunes, here printed; until a complete one comes up, I suggest that *both* fragments should be used, one after the other.

LOOK OUT BELOW!

This is by Thatcher, though a good deal altered in oral transmission. He used the tune, 'The Pirate King', printed in Anderson's *Colonial Ballads*. The version given here, both of tune and of words, is from *Singabout*, Vol. 1, No. 3.

THE MINER

One of the very few songs from the later period of gold-mining, after the alluvial gold was finished. This song from the deep-shaft mines was collected by the Folklore Society of Victoria from Mrs R. Sayers, late of Bulumwaal, Gippsland. I suspect that other singers will prefer to lengthen the two seven-bar phrases into eight-bar phrases.

3
THE BUSHRANGERS

BUSHRANGING, like the other arts, has its primitives, its classics, and its romantics. The primitives are the convict bushrangers, here represented by Jack Donahue.

Mr Meredith claims that 'The Wild Colonial Boy' is an off-shoot from one of the 'Bold Jack Donahue' ballads. Mr Frank Hardy on the other hand has found a good deal of evidence for the older view that the two ballads concern two different bushrangers: Donahue, an Irish-born transport, leader of a small gang, who was shot near Bringelly, N.S.W., on 1 September 1830; and Doolan, colonial-born at Monument Hill, near Castlemaine, Vic., who bailed up Judge Macoboy on the Bendigo Circuit in 1861, and was shot but not identified by the police shortly afterwards.

It is quite possible that the Doolan ballad was first sung to an existing Donahue tune, and thus came to share the same chorus. This would make it all the easier, as the new ballad spread northwards, for singers to confuse the famous Donahue with the unknown Doolan. The 'intermediate' versions quoted by Mr Meredith could thus be hybrids. Both ballads now have a great variety of tunes, some with chorus and some without.

The date 1861 is the date given by Boxall for the opening of the classic era of bushranging when the young colonials began to outdo their convict predecessors. The great classic hero is Ben Hall, a good man driven into outlawry by police persecution, chivalrous to women, dispensing his stolen gold to the folk of Canowindra and Binda in memorable sprees, killed on his feet in hopeless battle against seven assailants. The tunes of the Ben Hall ballads are outstandingly fine.

The dearth of ballads about the equally heroic Thunderbolt, even in his own district, is unaccountable unless by the supposition that large-scale capitalist farming broke up the old squatter communities before the ballads could take shape. The lack of ballads about Morgan, Scott, and the Clarkes is understandable: they were killers, not heroes.

Ned Kelly, the central romantic figure, was a killer too, and was hanged for it; but the ballads claim that he killed only in self-defence. He has been called 'the Brahms of bushranging', coming late in the succession and conscious of the weight of tradition on his shoulders. Unfortunately he became a hero to the Melbourne larrikins as well as to his own people, so that some of the Kelly ballads are quite unworthy of their subject. Many of the tunes are new-chum Irish, straight from the Dion Boucicault melodramas then playing at the Theatre Royal, Melbourne.

With Jack Bradshaw and his farcical 'robbery under reptiles' at Quirindi in 1880, romanticism turns towards decadence. There are legends in plenty about later bushrangers, but no more songs.

The notes to each song in this part are on page 76 of this book.

MY NAME IS BEN HALL

Rather slow

1. My name is Ben Hall, from Murrurundi I came;
The cause of my turn-out you all know the same.
I was sent to the gaol, my cattle turned to the Crown,
I was forced to the bush my sorrows to drown.

2. I was always well mounted, with a gun in my hand,
And I spoke people fair when I bid them to stand;
And I acted most gently towards all womankind
Tho' my false wife's behaviour was still in my mind.

3. I once met a squatter, I knew he had cash,
For the evening before he'd been cutting a dash;
But he handed straight over when my pistols I showed,
So I gave back five pounds he might spend on the road.

4. Here's a health to Frank Gardiner who's closely confined
And also Jack Vane who is serving his time!
With my friends in the bush I'll distribute this wealth,
And then I'll reserve my last shot for myself.

BOLD JACK DONAHUE

Fairly slow

There was a valiant highwayman of courage and renown, Who scorned to live in slavery or humble to the Crown: In Dublin City fair and free where first his breath he drew, 'Twas there they christened him the brave and bold Jack Donahue.

1. There was a valiant highwayman of courage and renown,
Who scorned to live in slavery or humble to the Crown;
In Dublin city fair and free where first his breath he drew,
'Twas there they christened him the brave and bold Jack Donahue.

2. He scarce had been transported unto the Australian shore,
When he took to the highway as he had done before;
And every week in the newspapers was published something new,
Concerning all the valiant deeds of bold Jack Donahue.

3. As Donahue was cruising one summer afternoon,
Little was his notion that his death would be so soon,
When to his surprise the horse-police appeared in his view,
And in quick time they did advance upon Jack Donahue.

4. The sergeant of the horse-police discharged his carabine,
And called aloud on Donahue to fight or to resign.
'I'd rather range these hills around like wolf or kangaroo,
Than work one hour for the government,' cried bold Jack Donahue.

5. Six rounds he fought the horse-police until the fatal ball,
Which pierced his heart with cruel smart caused Donahue to fall.
The sergeant and the corporal and all their cowardly crew,
It took them all their time to fall the bold Jack Donahue.

6. There were Freincy, Grant, bold Robin Hood and Brennan and O'Hare,
With Donahue the bushranger none of them could compare.
And now he's gone to heaven I hope with the saints and angels too,
May the Lord have mercy on the soul of bold Jack Donahue.

BOLD JACK DONAHUE
(another version)

Rather slow

If you'll but listen, a sorrowful tale I'll tell, Concerning a young hero in action lately fell: His name it was Jack Donahue of courage and renown, He'd scorn to live in slav-ry or be humbled to the Crown.

1. If you'll but listen, a sorrowful tale I'll tell,
Concerning a young hero in action lately fell;
His name it was Jack Donahoe of courage and renown,
He'd scorn to live in slavery or be humbled to the Crown.

2. On the twenty-fourth of August, it be his fatal day,
As he and his companions were cruising the highway,
He was hailed by the horse-police, he stood with heart and hand,
'Come on, my lads,' cried Donahoe, 'we'll fight them man for man.'
(One incomplete verse omitted)

3. 'Oh no,' says cowardly Walmsley, 'your laws we'll not fulfil.
You'll see there's eight or ten of them advancing on yon hill.
If it comes to an engagement, you'll rue it when too late,
So turn about and come with us – we'll form a quick retreat.'

4. 'Begone, you cowardly scoundrels, begone I pray from me!
For if we were united we'd gain this victory.
Today I'll fight with courage bold that all the world may see,
For I'd rather die in battle than be hung on a gallows tree.'

5. Soon they commenced their firing; poor Donahoe did say,
'My curse lay on you, Walmsley, for from me you've run away!'
The one played-off in front of him, the other at each side,
At length he received a mortal wound and in his glory died.

6. The equals of Jack Donahoe this country has never seen;
He did maintain his rights, my boys, and that right manfully.
He was chased about by hundreds for three long years or more,
Until at length the heavens decreed that he should roam no more.

7. The awful end of Donahoe, the truth to you I've told,
And hope that all good Christians will pray for his soul.
May holy angels guard him, likewise our Heavenly King,
And our Saviour Christ who died for us redeem his soul from sin.

THE WILD COLONIAL BOY

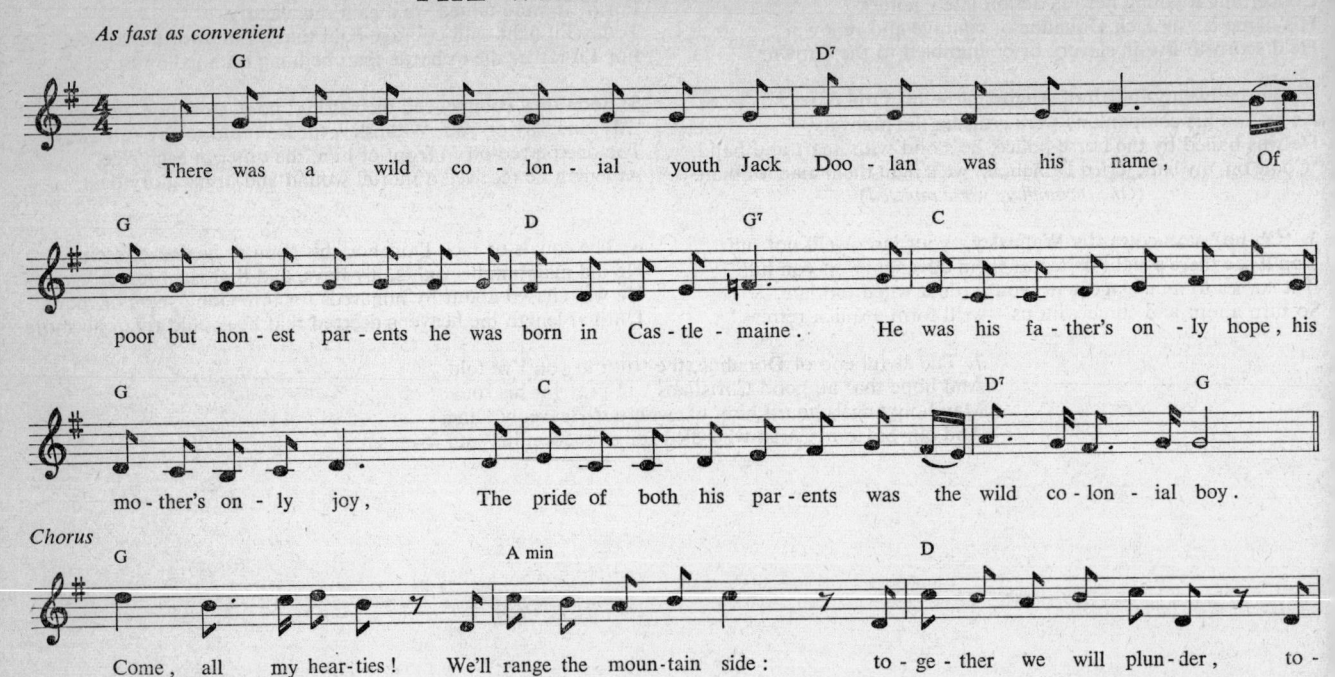

As fast as convenient

There was a wild co-lon-ial youth Jack Doo-lan was his name, Of poor but hon-est par-ents he was born in Cas-tle-maine. He was his fa-ther's on-ly hope, his mo-ther's on-ly joy, The pride of both his par-ents was the wild co-lon-ial boy.

Chorus

Come, all my hear-ties! We'll range the moun-tain side: to-ge-ther we will plun-der, to-ge - ther we will ride. We'll scour a - long the val - leys and gal - lop o'er the plains: We scorn to live in sla — ve — ry bound down with i — ron chains

Fairly quick *(another version)*

There was a wild co - lon - ial boy Jack Dow - ling was his name, Brought up by hon - est par — ents and born in Cas - tle - maine. He was his fa - ther's on - ly son, his mo - ther's pride and joy, And dear - ly dear - ly did they love this wild co - lon - ial boy.

1. There was a wild colonial youth, Jack Doolan was his name;
Of poor but honest parents he was born in Castlemaine.
He was his father's only hope, his mother's only joy;
The pride of both his parents was the wild colonial boy.

Chorus: Come, all my hearties! We'll range the mountain side;
Together we will plunder, together we will ride.
We'll scour along the valleys and gallop o'er the plains;
We scorn to live in slavery bowed down with iron chains.

2. He was barely sixteen years of age when he left his father's home,
And through Australia's sunny clime as a bushranger did roam.
He robbed those wealthy squatters, their stocks he did destroy,
A terror to the rich men was the wild colonial boy.

3. In sixty-one this daring youth commenced his wild career;
With a heart that knew no danger, no foeman did he fear.
He held the Beechworth mail-coach up, and robbed Judge Macoboy,
Who trembled and gave up his gold to the wild colonial boy.

4. He bade the Judge good-morning, and told him to beware
For he'd never rob a decent judge that acted on the square,
But not to rob a mother of her son and only joy
Or you'll breed a race of outlaws like the wild colonial boy.

5. One day as he was riding the mountain-side along,
A-listening to the little birds their pleasant laughing song,
Three mounted troopers came in sight, Kelly, Davis and Fitzroy,
And thought that they would capture him, the wild colonial boy.

6. 'Surrender now, Jack Doolan! You see we're three to one.
Surrender now, Jack Doolan, you daring highwayman!'
But he drew a pistol from his belt and spun it like a toy:
'I'll fight but I won't surrender,' said the wild colonial boy.

7. He fired at Trooper Kelly and brought him to the ground,
And in return from Davis received a mortal wound;
All shattered through the jaws he lay still firing at Fitzroy.
And that's the way they captured the wild colonial boy.

BALLAD OF BEN HALL'S GANG

Tune: a relative of "The Black Horse"

Dignified march time

Come all you sons of liberty and listen to my tale: A story of bush-ranging days I will to you un-veil. 'Tis of those valiant heroes, God bless them one and all! Let us sit and sing "God save the King, Dunn, Gilbert and Ben Hall."

BALLAD OF BEN HALL'S GANG
(another version)

Tune: one of those to "William Riley"

March time

Come all you sons of liberty and listen to my tale: A story of bush-ranging days I will to you unveil. 'Tis of those valiant heroes, God bless them one and all! Let us sit and sing "God save the King, Dunn, Gilbert and Ben Hall."

1. Come all you sons of liberty and listen to my tale;
A story of bushranging days I will to you unveil.
'Tis of those valiant heroes, God bless them one and all!
Let us sit and sing: 'God save the King, Dunn, Gilbert and Ben Hall.'

2. Ben Hall he was a squatter, and he owned six hundred head;
A peaceful, quiet man was he until he met Sir Fred.
The troopers burnt his homestead down, his cattle perished all.
'I've all my sentence yet to earn,' was the word of brave Ben Hall.

3. John Gilbert was a flash cove, and young O'Meally too,
With Ben and Bourke and Dunn and Vane, they all were comrades true.
They bailed the Carcoar mailcoach up and made the troopers crawl.
There's a thousand pound set on the heads of Dunn, Gilbert and Ben Hall.

4. From Bathurst down to Goulburn town they made the coaches stand,
While far behind, Sir Frederick's men went labouring thro' the land.
Then at Canowindra's best hotel they gave a public ball:
'We don't hurt them that don't hurt us,' says Dunn, Gilbert and Ben Hall.

5. They held the gold-commissioner to ransom on the spot,
But young John Vane surrendered after Mickey Bourke was shot.
O'Meally at Goimbla did like a hero fall;
But 'We'll take the country over yet,' says Dunn, Gilbert and Ben Hall.

6. They never robbed a needy man, the records go to show,
But staunch and loyal to their mates, unflinching to the foe;
So we'll drink a toast tonight, my lads, their memories to recall.
Let us sit and sing: 'God save the King, Dunn, Gilbert and Ben Hall!'

FRANK GARDINER

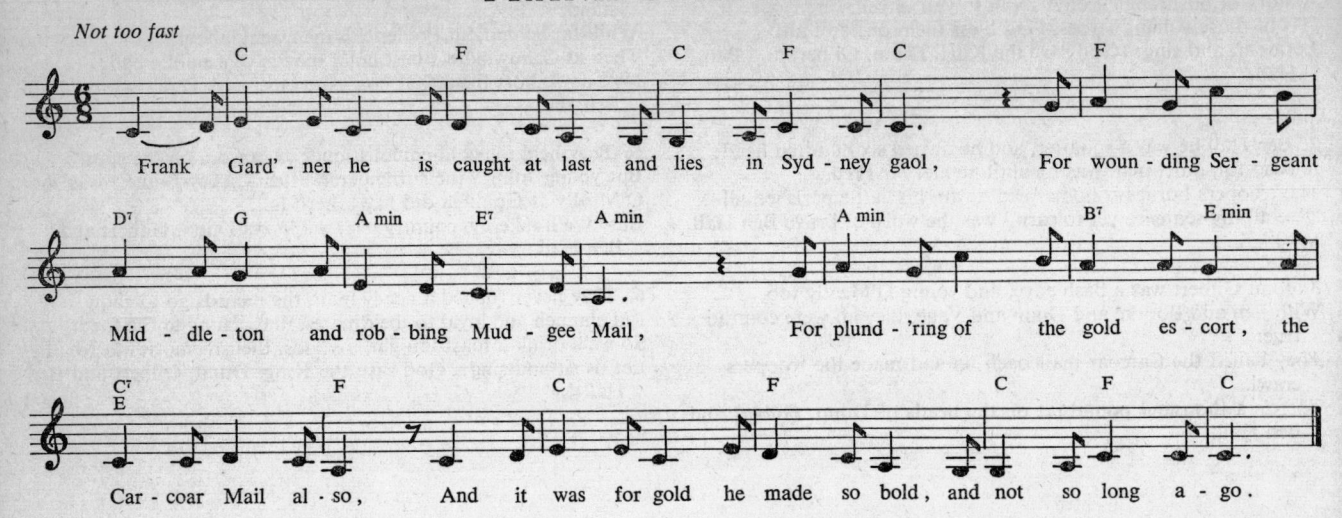

Not too fast

Frank Gard'ner he is caught at last and lies in Sydney gaol, For wounding Sergeant Middleton and robbing Mudgee Mail, For plund'ring of the gold escort, the Carcoar Mail also, And it was for gold he made so bold, and not so long ago.

1. Frank Gardiner he is caught at last, he lies in Sydney gaol,
For wounding Sergeant Middleton and robbing Mudgee Mail,
For plundering of the Gold Escort, the Carcoar Mail also,
And it was for gold he made so bold, and not so long ago.

2. His daring deeds surprised them all throughout the Sydney land,
And on his friends he gave a call and quickly raised a band,
And fortune always favoured him until the time of late,
Until Ben Hall and Gilbert met with their dreadful fate.

3. Farewell adieu to outlawed Frank, he was the poor man's friend,
The Government has secured him, the laws he did offend.
He boldly stood his trial and answered in a breath:
'And do what you will, you can but kill. I have no fear of death.'

4. Day after day they remanded him, escorted from the bar,
Fresh charges brought against him from neighbours near and far,
And now it is all over, the sentence they have passed,
All sought to find a verdict and 'Guilty' 'twas at last.

5. O'Meally has surrendered, Ben Hall's got his death wound,
And as for Johnnie Gilbert, near Binalong was found,
Alone he was and lost his horse, three troopers came in sight,
And they fought the three most manfully, got slaughtered in the fight.

6. When lives you take, a warning, boys, a woman never trust,
She will turn round, I will be bound, Queen's evidence the first,
He's doing two and thirty years, he's doomed to serve the crown,
And well may he say, he cursed the day he met with Mrs Brown.

59

THE STREETS OF FORBES

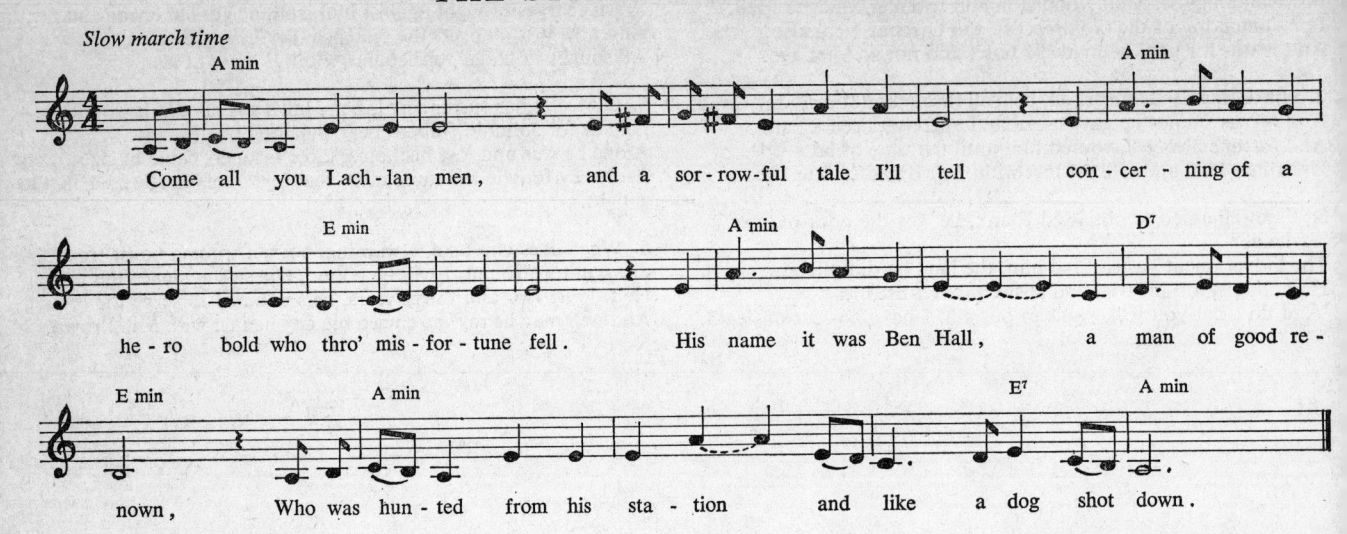

Slow march time

Come all you Lach-lan men, and a sor-row-ful tale I'll tell con-cer-ning of a he-ro bold who thro' mis-for-tune fell. His name it was Ben Hall, a man of good re-nown, Who was hun-ted from his sta-tion and like a dog shot down.

1. Come all you Lachlan men, and a sorrowful tale I'll tell
Concerning of a hero bold who through misfortune fell.
His name it was Ben Hall, a man of good renown
Who was hunted from his station, and like a dog shot down.

2. Three years he roamed the roads, and he showed the traps some fun;
A thousand pound was on his head, with Gilbert and John Dunn.
Ben parted from his comrades, the outlaws did agree
To give away bushranging and to cross the briny sea.

3. Ben went to Goobang Creek, and that was his downfall;
For riddled like a sieve was valiant Ben Hall.
'Twas early in the morning upon the fifth of May
When the seven police surrounded him as fast asleep he lay.

4. Bill Dargin he was chosen to shoot the outlaw dead;
The troopers then fired madly, and filled him full of lead.
They rolled him in a blanket, and strapped him to his prad,
And led him through the streets of Forbes to show the prize they had.

THE DEATH OF BEN HALL

As if it were a slow

Come all you young Australians, and hear what did befall concerning of a decent man whose name was bold Ben Hall. An outcast of society, he was forced to take the road, Along of how his faithless wife cleared out from his abode.

1. Come all you young Australians, and hear what did befall
Concerning of a decent man whose name was bold Ben Hall.
An outcast of society he was forced to take the road
Along of how his faithless wife cleared out from his abode.

2. The traps pursued him like a dog through every hill and dale,
Until he faced his enemies and made them all turn tail.
No petty, mean or pilfering act would bold Ben Hall endure;
He preyed on rich and hearty men, and scorned to rob the poor.

3. One night as he in hiding lay upon the Lachlan Plain,
The troopers had surrounded him, his courage was in vain,
And when he stirred to ease himself, not knowing who was by,
Without a word of warning the bullets fast did fly.

4. Although he had a lion's heart, the bravest of the brave,
They riddled him with thirty wounds, no word of challenge gave;
And cowardly-hearted Condell, the Sergeant of Police,
Crept up and fired with famous glee which gave him his release.

5. Throughout Australia's sunny clime Ben Hall will range no more;
His fame is spread from far and near to every distant shore;
And generations after this his name will yet recall
And tell their children of the deeds committed by Ben Hall.

MY NAME IS EDWARD KELLY

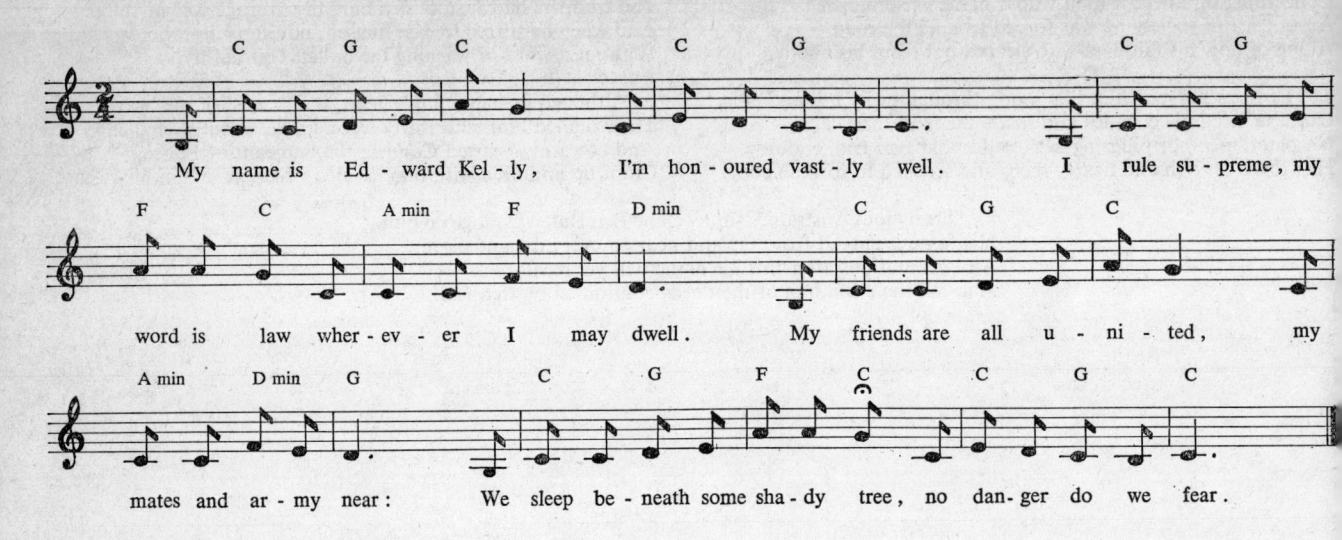

My name is Edward Kelly, I'm honoured vastly well. I rule supreme, my word is law wherever I may dwell. My friends are all united, my mates and army near: We sleep beneath some shady tree, no danger do we fear.

1. My name is Edward Kelly, I'm honoured vastly well.
I rule supreme, my word is law, wherever I may dwell.
My friends are all united, my mates and army near;
We sleep beneath some shady tree, no danger do we fear.

2. Now the first of my adventures was through my sister dear,
Who was grossly insulted and put in bodily fear;
And when I came to hear of this it made my heart to ache;
I took to the hills to have revenge, all for my sister's sake.

3. Oh I am young and in my prime, I'm twenty-four years old.
I spent some time in vanity among young girls so bold;
But now I am a-robbing, and loudly my guns do roar.
'Twas there I shot poor Kennedy, which grieved my heart full sore.

4. In Mansfield that fair township where I was bred and born,
Oft times have I roamed those hills from dark till early morn,
But now I am a-robbing upon the Queen's Highway;
We fight the traps and rob the banks, and quickly slip away.

5. Now the troopers they are all sent out to search the country round,
To bring in this notorious gang, but the Kellys can't be found.
The Kellys are in the ridges, the police in ranks abound;
The price upon my head, my boys, is now one thousand pound.

6. I never would surrender to any coat of blue,
Or any man that wears a crown belonging to the crew.
They're game, there is no doubt of it, when they are on the beat,
But it took ten traps to take Ben Hall when he was fast asleep.

7. I'd rather die like Donahue, that bushranger so brave,
Than be taken by the Government to be treated like a slave.
I'ld rather fight with all my might as long as I'd eyes to see;
I'ld rather die ten thousand deaths than die on the gallows tree.

8. Now all young men take my advice, that's bent on a roving life;
Pray do not roam but stay at home, settle down and take a wife.
For if you go a-robbing upon the Queen's Highway
You'll have to fight with all your might, or else lay down and die.

NED KELLY'S FAREWELL TO GRETA

Farewell my home in Greta, my sister Kate farewell: It grieves my heart to leave you, but here I cannot dwell.

(*another version*)

Farewell my home in Greta, my sister Kate farewell: It grieves my heart to leave you, but here I cannot dwell. The brand of Cain is

66

on my brow, the blood-hounds on my trail, and for the sake of gol-den gain my free-dom they as-sail. Fare-well fare-well to Gre — ta.

Chorus or accompaniment

1. NED: Farewell my home in Greta, my sister Kate farewell;
   It grieves my heart to leave you, but here I cannot dwell.
   The brand of Cain is on my brow, the bloodhounds on my trail,
   And for the sake of golden gain my freedom they assail.

2. But should they cross my chequered path, by all I hold on earth,
   I'll give them cause to rue the day their mothers gave them birth.
   I'll shoot them down like kangaroos that roam the forests wide,
   And leave their bodies bleaching upon some woodland side.

3. KATE: Oh Edward, dearest brother, you know you must not go
   And risk to be encountered by such a mighty foe!
   It's duly North lies Morgan's Tower, and pointing to the sky
   South-east and East the mighty range of Gippsland mountains lie.

4. You know the country well, dear Ned, go take your comrades there,
   And profit by your knowledge of the wombat and the bear.
   And let no petty quarrels part the union of our gang,
   But stick to one another, Ned, and guard our brother Dan.

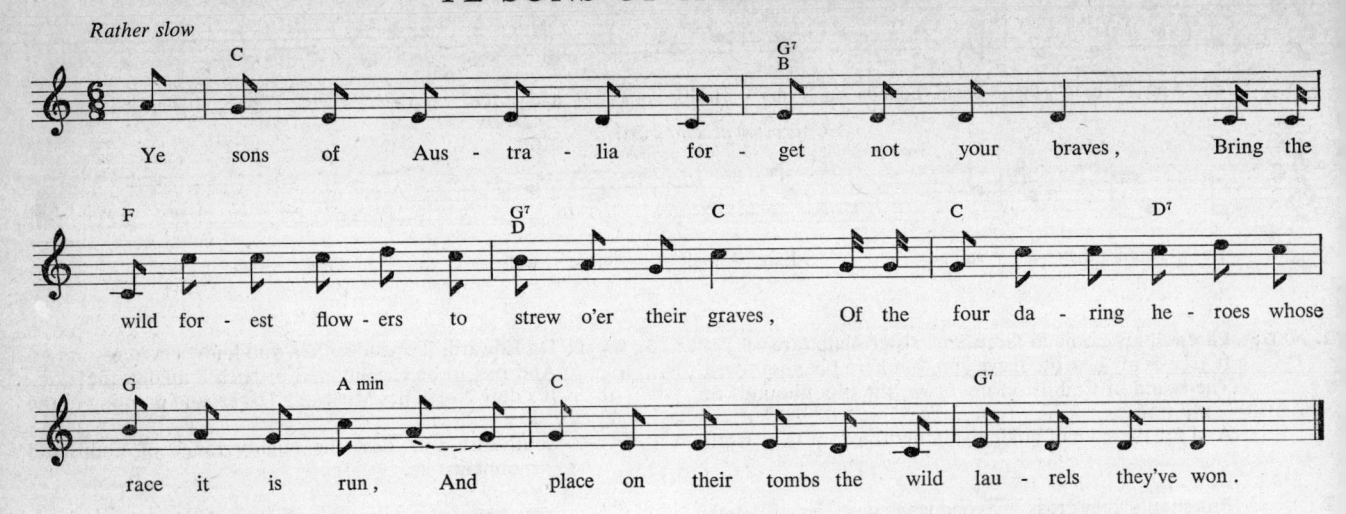

YE SONS OF AUSTRALIA

Rather slow

Ye sons of Australia forget not your braves, Bring the wild forest flowers to strew o'er their graves, Of the four daring heroes whose race it is run, And place on their tombs the wild laurels they've won.

1. Ye sons of Australia forget not your braves,
Bring the wild forest flowers to strew o'er their graves,
Of the four daring outlaws whose race it is run,
And place on their tombs the wild laurels they've won.

2. On the banks of Euroa they made their first rush,
They cleared out at Coppies, then steered through the bush,
Black trackers and troopers soon did them pursue
But cast out their anchor when near them they drew.

3. The daring Kate Kelly how noble her mien
As she sat on her horse like an Amazon queen,
She rode through the forest revolver at hand,
Regardless of danger, who dare bid her stand.

4. May the angels protect this young heroine bold
And her name be recorded in letters of gold,
Though her brothers were outlaws, she loved them most dear,
And hastened to tell them when danger was near.

5. But the great God of Mercy who scans all her ways
Commanded grim death to shorten their days,
Straightway to Glenrowan their course he did steer
To slay those bold outlaws and stop their career.

6. The daring Ned Kelly came forth from the inn,
To wreak his last vengeance he then did begin,
To slaughter the troopers straightway he did go,
And tore up the railway their train to o'erthrow.

7. But the great God of Mercy, to baulk his intent,
And stop the destruction, a messenger sent,
A person named Curnow, who seemed in great dread,
Cried out to the troopers, 'There's danger ahead!'

8. But Time hath its changes; how dreadful their fate,
They found out their error when it was too late.
The house was surrounded by troopers two-score,
And also expected a great many more.

9. The daring Ned Kelly, revolver in hand,
Came to the verandah, the troopers he scanned,
Said he 'You cursed wretches, we do you defy,
We will not surrender, we conquer or die.'

10. Like the free sons of Ishmael, brought up in the wilds,
Amongst forests and mountains, and rocky defiles
These brave lawless fellows could not be controlled,
And fought ten to one, until death we are told.

11. Next day at Glenrowan, how dreadful the doom,
Of Hart and Dan Kelly shut up in a room,
A trooper named Johnson, set the house all aflame
To burn those bold outlaws, it was a great shame.

12. The daring Kate Kelly came forth from the crowd,
And on her poor brother she called out aloud,
'Come forth my dear brother, and fight while you can,'
But a ball had just taken the life of poor Dan.

13. Next morning our hero came forth from the bush
Encased in strong armour his way he did push.
To gain his bold comrades it was his desire –
The troopers espied him, and soon opened fire.

14. The bullets bound off him just like a stone wall,
His fiendish appearance soon did them appal.
His legs unprotected a trooper soon found,
And a shot well directed brought him to the ground.

15. Now he arose captured, and stripped off his mail,
Well guarded by troopers and taken to gaol.
Addicted for murder, it grieved him full sore.
His friends and relations his fate may deplore.

16. Now, all you young fellows take warning by me,
Beware of bushranging, and bad company,
For like many others you may feel the dart
Which pierced the two Kellys, Joe Byrne, and Steve Hart.

STRINGYBARK CREEK

Tune: "Paddy Fagan"

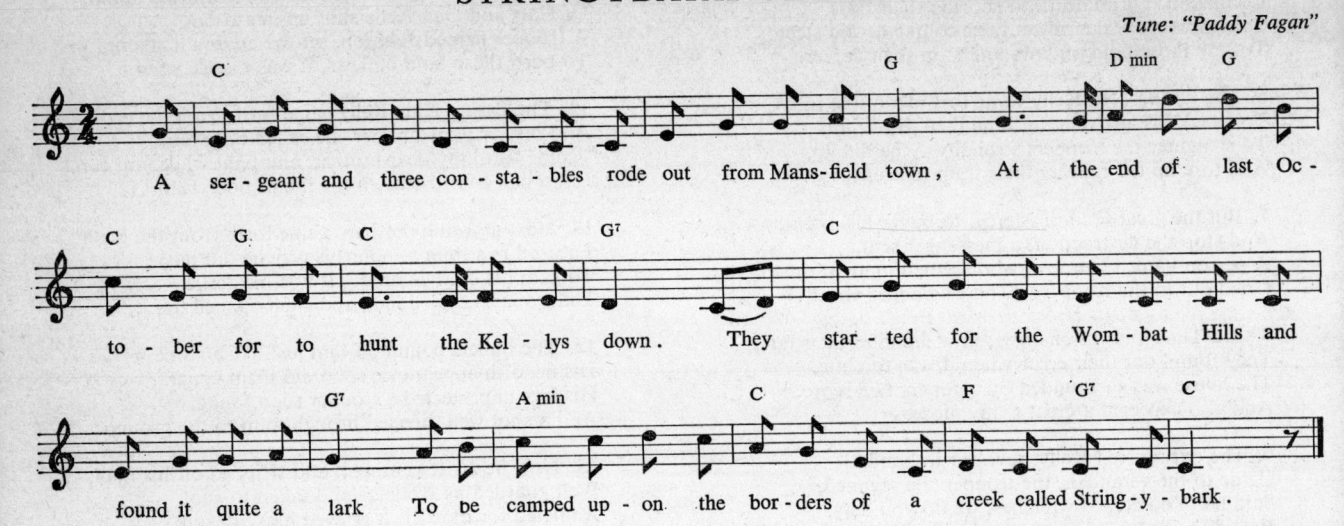

A sergeant and three constables rode out from Mansfield town, At the end of last October for to hunt the Kellys down. They started for the Wombat Hills and found it quite a lark To be camped upon the borders of a creek called Stringybark.

STRINGYBARK CREEK
(another version)

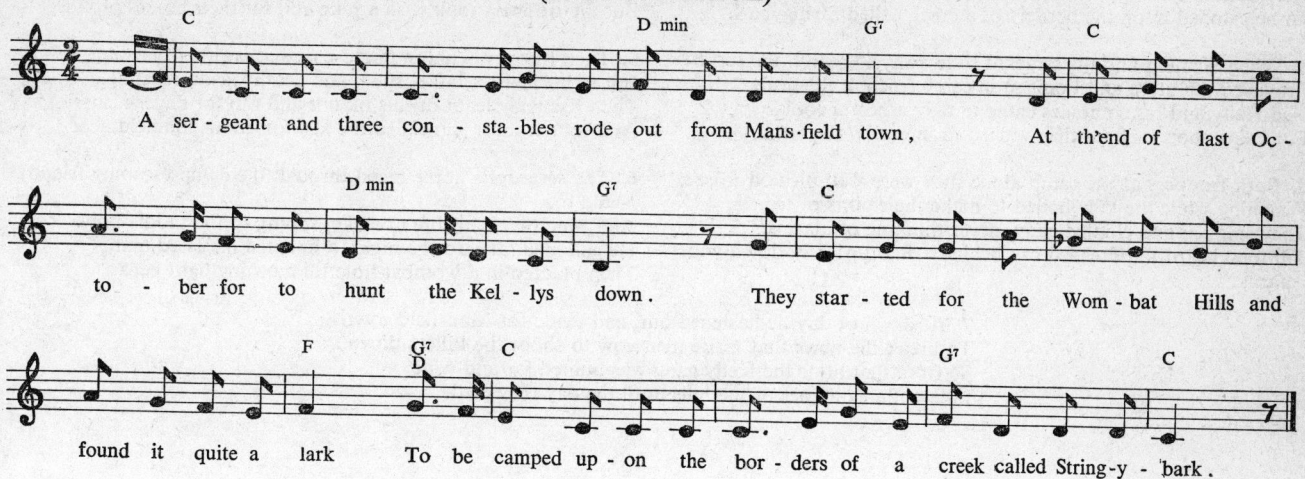

A sergeant and three constables rode out from Mansfield town, At th'end of last October for to hunt the Kellys down. They started for the Wombat Hills and found it quite a lark To be camped upon the borders of a creek called Stringybark.

1. A sergeant and three constables rode out from Mansfield town
At the end of last October for to hunt the Kellys down.
They started for the Wombat Hills, and found it quite a lark
To be camped upon the borders of a creek called Stringybark.

2. When Scanlon and the sergeant rode away to search the scrub
Leaving MacIntyre and Lonigan in camp to cook the grub,
Ned Kelly and his comrades came to take a nearer look,
For being short of flour they wished to interview the cook.

3. Both troopers at the camp alone they were well pleased to see,
Watching while the billy boiled to make their pints of tea.
They smoked and chatted gaily, never thinking of alarms,
Till they heard the dreaded cry behind: 'Bail up! Lay down your arms!'

4. It was later in the afternoon, the sergeant and his mate
Came riding blithely through the bush to meet their cruel fate.
'The Kellys have the drop on you,' the prisoners cried aloud,
But the troopers took it as a joke and sat their horses proud.

5. Then trooper Scanlon made a move his rifle to unsling,
But to his heart a bullet sped, and death was in its sting.
Then Kennedy leapt off his mount and ran for cover near,
And fought most gamely to the last for all his life held dear.

6. The sergeant's horse raced through the camp escaping friend and foe,
And MacIntyre, his life at stake, sprang to the saddle-bow.
He galloped far into the night, a haunted harassed man,
Then planted in a wombat-hole till morning light began.

7. At dawn of day he hastened out, and made for Mansfield town
To break the news that made men vow to shoot the killers down.
So from that hour the Kelly gang was hunted far and wide
Like outlaw dingoes of the hills until the day they died.

THE BALLAD OF KELLY'S GANG

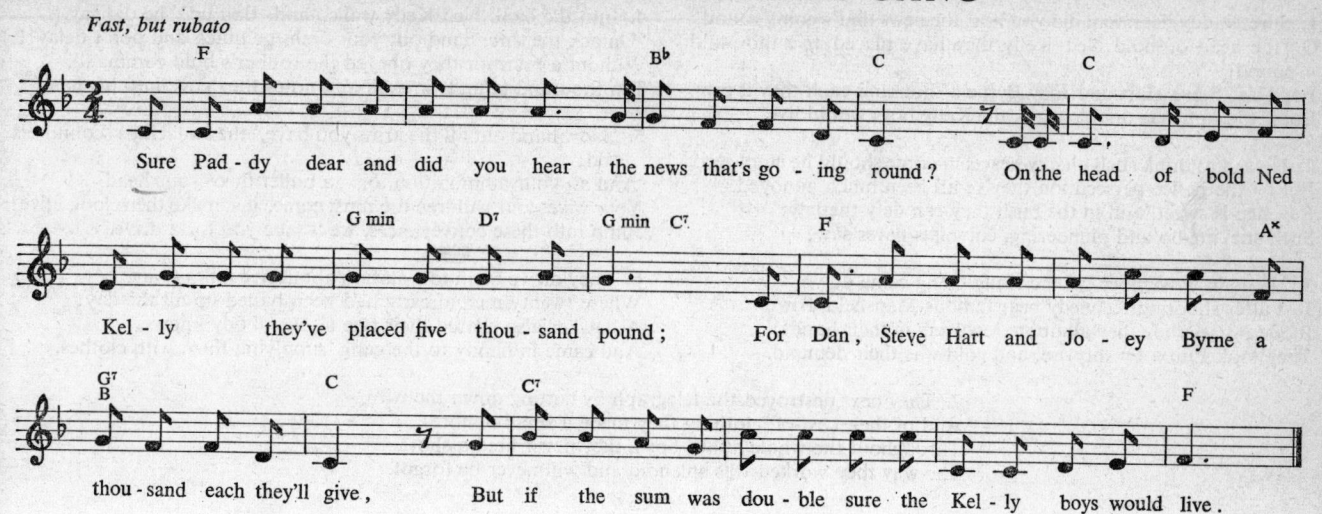

Fast, but rubato

Sure Pad-dy dear and did you hear the news that's go-ing round? On the head of bold Ned Kel-ly they've placed five thou-sand pound; For Dan, Steve Hart and Jo-ey Byrne a thou-sand each they'll give, But if the sum was dou-ble sure the Kel-ly boys would live.

Part I

1. Sure, Paddy dear, and did you hear the news that's going round?
On the head of bold Ned Kelly they have placed five thousand pound;
For Dan, Steve Hart and Joey Byrne a thousand each they'll give,
But if the sum was double, sure, the Kelly boys would live.

2. It's sad to think such plucky hearts in crime should be employed,
But by the police persecution they've all been much annoyed.
Revenge is sweet, and in the bush they can defy the law:
Such sticking-up and plundering, colonials never saw!

3. 'Twas in November '78 the Kelly Gang came down,
Just after shooting Kennedy near famous Mansfield Town.
Blood horses rode they all upon, revolvers in their hands;
They took Euroa by surprise, and gold was their demand.

4. Into the bank Ned Kelly walks, and 'Bail up!' he did say,
'Unlock the safe, hand out your cash, be quick and don't delay!'
Without a murmur they obeyed the robber's bold command,
Ten thousand pounds in gold and notes they gave into his hand.

5. 'Now hand out all the arms you have,' the audacious scoundrels said;
'And all your ammunition, or – a bullet thro' your head.
Your wives and children too must come, just make them look alive!
Jump into these conveyances, we'll take you for a drive.'

6. They drove them to a station about five miles away,
Where twenty men already had been bailed up all the day;
A hawker also shared their fate as everybody knows,
And came in handy to the gang, supplying them with clothes.

7. They next destroyed the telegraph by cutting down the wire,
And of their cast-off clothing they made a small bonfire.
Throughout the whole affair, boys, they never fired a shot:
The way they worked was splendid and will never be forgot.

Part II

8. O Paddy dear, do shed a tear, I can't but sympathize!
These Kellys are a terror, and they've made another rise:
This time across the billabong, on Morgan's ancient beat,
They've robbed the bank of thousands and in safety did retreat.

9. They rode into Jerilderie town at twelve o'clock at night,
And rose the troopers from their beds all in a dreadful fright.
They took them in their nightshirts, ashamed am I to tell;
They covered them with revolvers, and locked them in a cell.

10. Next morning being Sunday, of course they must be good;
They dressed themselves in troopers' clothes and Neddy chopped some wood.
Nobody there suspected them; for troopers all they pass;
And Dan, the most religious, took the Sergeant's wife to Mass.

11. They spent the day most pleasantly, had plenty of good cheer,
Beef steaks and onions, tomato sauce and beer.
The lady in attendance indulged in pleasant talk,
And just to ease the troopers' wives they took them for a walk.

12. On Monday morning early, still masters of the ground,
They took their horses to the forge and got them shod all round.
Then back they brought and mounted them, they plan the raid so well,
And in company with the troopers they stuck up the Royal Hotel.

13. They shouted freely for all hands and paid for all they drank;
Then two of them remained in charge and two went to the bank.
They bailed up all the bankers' clerks and robbed them of their gold,
And caught the manager in his bath, all blue with funk and cold.

14. They destroyed communication by telegraph at last.
Of robberies and plunderings they had a perfect fast.
Where they have gone's a mystery, the police they cannot tell,
So until we hear from them again I'll bid ye's all farewell.

NOTES

MY NAME IS BEN HALL

A composite for which I take responsibility. I was given the words as a recitation, while touring on adult education business in New England. They are a cut down version of those given in Paterson's *Old Bush Songs*. The tune is one much played by bush fiddlers as a *varsoviana*, and called 'The Dear Irish Boy'. I am bound to point out that the phrase which occurs in Paterson's version 'from Uranga I come' is quite historically incorrect. When I sang the ballad in that form to schoolchildren in New England, they told me that Murrurundi was really Hall's birthplace, and asked me to make the substitution.

BOLD JACK DONAHUE

The first version is from *Bandicoot Ballads*: the text mainly from Miss Kath Watson, Lindum; the tune is from Mrs Anderson, Lota, who had it from her father, a drover. The other version is from Meredith's excellent pamphlet *The Wild Colonial Boy*. The incomplete verse omitted from the singing text runs as follows:

> Says he to his companions, 'Now if you're only game –
> You'll see there's only three of them, our number's just the same.
> For today it's life or liberty, or fall upon the plain.'

I wish I had space for one of the versions that includes the fine couplet:

> And as he closed his bloodshot eyes to bid the world adieu,
> 'I'll never humble to the Crown!' cried bold Jack Donahue.

Other tunes and other verses are given in Anderson's *Colonial Ballads* (but without source or singer) and by Meredith in the work already quoted. Paterson, of course, gives verses but not tunes. The chorus lines, shared with the next ballad, are not often heard today, though they belong originally to this ballad.

THE WILD COLONIAL BOY

First tune from *Bandicoot Ballads*. I learnt it in childhood, chorus and all; and was startled when I met the verse-tune in *The Beggars' Opera*. The chorus appears to be purely home-grown, and turns up in a Queensland version as well as in this Victorian tune. In many other versions, the chorus lines are sung to a repeat of the tune, as they are in the second one given here. The other tune is from Theo. Archdeacon, Inglewood, Western Australia, and is printed in *Singabout*, Vol. 3, No. 3, and in Meredith's book.

Still further tunes are in *Singabout*, Vol. 3, No. 3; in Frank Clune's *Rolling Down the Lachlan*; in Palmer and Sutherland's *Old Australian Bush Ballads*, and in *The Overlander Songbook* ('Wearing of the Green').

BALLAD OF BEN HALL'S GANG

This ballad has been the source and the recipient of a good deal of line-swapping and confusion. A remarkably long and complete version (eleven stanzas) is given in Frank Clune's *Wild Colonial Boys*, incorporating lines from an amusing but 'un-bushy' ballad 'John Gilbert'. Paterson accepted an obviously confused version of this with a ballad that has disappeared from view, about Hall's escape from the police near Binalong on 28 May 1863. He also printed the 'John Gilbert' mentioned above. They are worth looking up.

Take this as a singable composite. It was assembled from the collections and recollections of the entire *Bandicoot* ensemble, and their friends and acquaintances, for concert use. Tune 1 is from Mrs Raymond and Brenton Wilson, Wynnum. Tune 2 is from T. J. Lyne, now of King Island, Bass Strait. A tune very like Tune 1 is given in *The Overlander Songbook*; it is Irish and known variously as 'The Airy Bachelor' and 'The Black Horse'.

FRANK GARDINER

Given in rather a mangled form by Jack Bradshaw. John Meredith has corrected Bradshaw's version by using lines and verses supplied by Mrs Popplewell. The tune is said to be one of those to 'Rise Up Now, William Riley'.

THE STREETS OF FORBES

The poem was written – or at any rate written down – by Hall's brother-in-law John McGuire, an eye-witness of the ghastly procession. This version, differing in a few lines (for the better, I think) was sung to me in the back room of a Brisbane pub by a Mrs Ewell, late of Bathurst. McGuire's manuscript has been reprinted by Clune and by Stewart and Keesing.

THE DEATH OF BEN HALL

Several ballads exist with this title, including one too long for singing. Several persons have assured me that this was written by Will Ogilvie. The tune is from *Speewah*, Vol. 1, No. 2, taken down by John Meredith from the singing of Mrs Sloane, Lithgow, New South Wales. The words given here are a condensation or abbreviation of the original words in *Speewah*. If it is felt that the accompaniment is wrong, try singing this ballad over a pure drone D, bagpipe fashion. Really I think it would be most difficult to accompany the tune properly.

MY NAME IS EDWARD KELLY

Collected by the Queensland Folklore Society, and published for the first time in the *Queensland Pocket Songbook*.

NED KELLY'S FAREWELL TO GRETA

Tune 1 and text (with very few amendments) were recorded by the Folklore Society of Victoria from the singing of Mrs C. S. Peatey, Brunswick, Victoria. A fuller version of the words, collected by Max Brown from Mrs Barry, Beechworth, is printed in Stewart and Keesing's *Old Bush Songs*. Very similar words are printed in *Songs from the Kelly Country*, to a 'Denis O'Riley' tune. The alternative tune given here was learnt by Mr Albert Nord, Belmont, Queensland, from a Danish shipmate in his seagoing days.

YE SONS OF AUSTRALIA

From *Songs from the Kelly Country*. Mr C. McComish, late of Boggabilla, New South Wales, has been trying for years to give me a different tune, but his memory always fails in the presence of other people, so I cannot supply it. The original text is in sixteen stanzas. I have reduced it here, as audiences are less patient these days.

STRINGYBARK CREEK

There are many versions of this ballad, some almost farcical, some serious and tragic. I have taken what seems to be the most sustained and unitary version of the words, collected early in the 1890s in the Strathbogie Ranges by the late W. J. Wye. The tunes given are (1) from the Sydney Bush Music Club publication, *Songs from the Kelly Country*, where it is named 'Paddy Fagan' and (2) from the fiddle-tune 'Stringybark Creek'. *The Overlander Songbook* uses 'The Wearing of the Green'.

THE BALLAD OF KELLY'S GANG

This very intelligently condensed version was recorded by the Folklore Society of Victoria from the singing of Mr Tom Fox, Kanumbra, Victoria. The division into Parts I and II is just an editorial suggestion; and I have had to do a little patchwork with some verses which Mr Fox left incomplete. The fullest known version is in *Songs from the Kelly Country*, where the tune is simply 'The Wearing of the Green'.

I once met in Brisbane the daughter of the girl who poured drinks for Ned Kelly at 'the hotel' (was it Davidsons or The Royal Mail?) on the occasion of the Jerilderie Raid. But Professor Letters of the University of New England goes one better: he has shaken the hand of a man who once shook the hand of Kate Kelly!

4
PASTORAL AUSTRALIA

This section has no coherence, I warn you, and its boundary on the far side is barely surveyed. It takes in the homestead, the bachelor-quarters, the hut, and even the black's camp; and, far below the blacks in the eyes of the squatter and the stockmen, it takes in the free-selector too.

Free-selection was planned by John Robertson and other statesmen to create an 'industrious peasantry' on land formerly leased to squatters. What it actually created was something like civil war in the back blocks and a wealthy class of landsharks in Sydney and Melbourne.

The unfortunate free-selector and the new-chum jackaroo succeeded together to the post of butt, formerly held by the new-chum digger. Conscious of a stigma on his name, the jackaroo liked to call himself a stockman, particularly in his own songs. There is no parallel case, however, of a selector trying to pass himself off as a squatter; and in any case selectors had no spare time for singing. The sons of the selectors normally rose out of the butt class by going off shearing or droving.

The notes to each song in this part are on page 110 of this book.

MUSTERING DAY

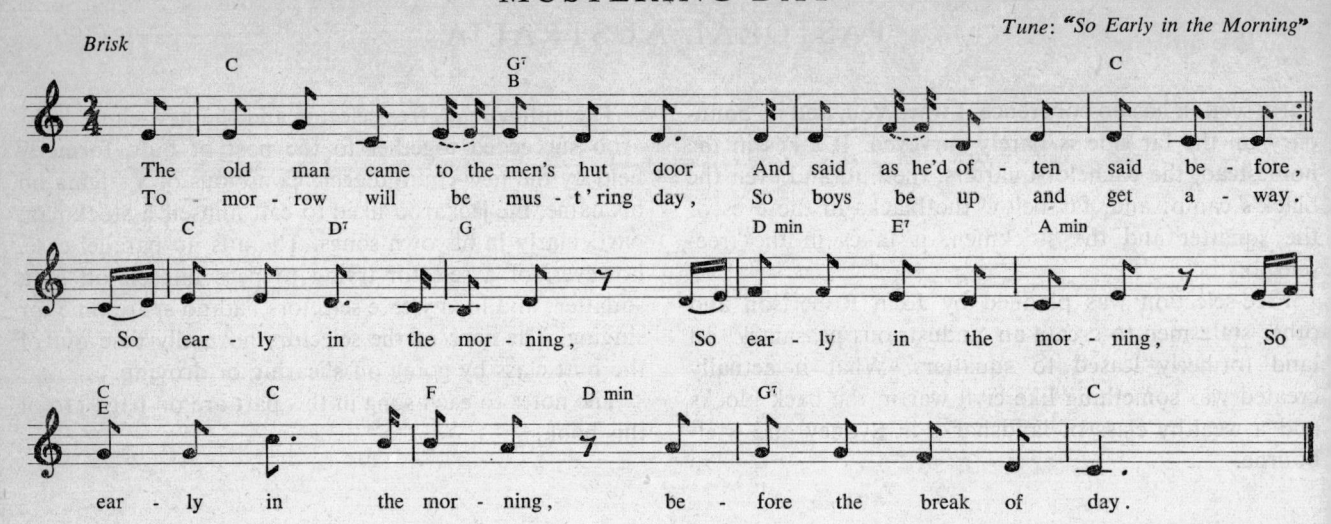

Tune: "So Early in the Morning"

The old man came to the men's hut door, And said as he'd often said before,
To-morrow will be must'ring day, So boys be up and get away.
So early in the morning, So early in the morning, So early in the morning, before the break of day.

1. The old man came to the men's hut door
And said as he'd often said before:
'Tomorrow will be mustering day,
So boys be up and get away.'

Chorus: So early in the morning (*three times*)
　　　　Before the break of day.

2. So up we got before sunrise
And off to breakfast with sleepy eyes;
The horses soon were caught and manned,
And on we jumped with whip in hand.

3. We found a mob not far away,
And started them off without delay.
A poley cow ran on the track;
The old man rode to fetch her back.

4. Now the mare he rode was fast and free,
And ran him against a bluegum tree.
She threw the old man on his head,
We picked him up and found him dead.

5. Next day I got the big draught horse
To take away the old man's corpse;
And in the dawn's uncertain light
I got a most tremendous fright.

6. For there I saw the old man's ghost
Sitting on the stockyard's corner post.
Smoking the very same old clay
He used to smoke on mustering day.

7. Where'er I go, where'er I stray,
I'll never forget that mustering day,
I'll never forget the old man's ghost
With his black dudgeen on the stockyard post.

THE DYING STOCKMAN

Fairly slow waltz

A strapping young stockman lay dying, A saddle supporting his head. And his comrades around him were crying As he leant on his elbow and

Chorus

said: "Wrap me up in my stockwhip and blanket, and bury me deep down below, where the dingoes and crows will not find me, In the shade where the coolibahs grow.

* *see p.110*

82

THE DYING STOCKMAN
(another version)

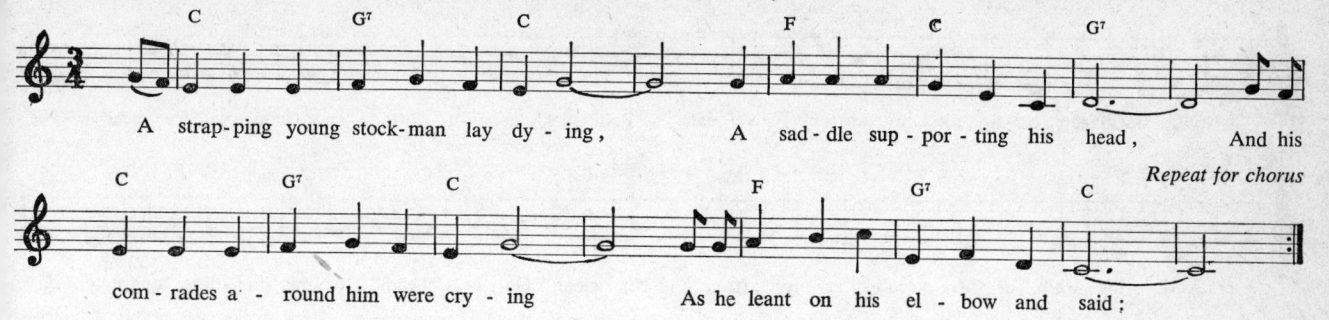

A strapping young stockman lay dying, A saddle supporting his head, And his comrades around him were crying As he leant on his elbow and said:

Repeat for chorus

1. A strapping young stockman lay dying,
A saddle supporting his head;
And his comrades around him were crying
As he leant on his elbow and said:

Chorus: Wrap me up in my stockwhip and blanket
And bury me deep down below,
Where the dingoes and crows will not find me,
In the shade where the coolibahs grow.

2. Cut down a couple of saplings,
Place one at my head and my toe;
Carve on them a stockwhip and saddle
To show there's a stockman below.

3. There's some tea in that battered old billy,
Place the pannikins all in a row,
And we'll drink to the next merry meeting,
In the place where all good stockmen go.

4. I hear the wail of a dingo,
In the gloom of the scrubs down below,
And he rings the knell of a stockman,
Farewell, dear old pals, I must go.

5. If I had the wings of a pigeon,
Far over the plains I would fly;
I'd fly to the arms of my loved ones,
And there I would lay down and die.

THE STOCKMAN'S LAST BED

Be ye stock-men or no, to my sto-ry give ear. Poor Jack's gone a-loft, no more shall we hear The crack of his whip or his steed's live-ly trot, His clear "Go a-head" or his jing-ling quart-pot.

Chorus

We laid him where wat-tles their sweet fra-grance shed, And the tall gum trees sha-dow, the tall gum trees sha-dow And the tall gum trees sha-dow the stock-man's last bed.

84

THE STOCKMAN'S LAST BED
(another version)

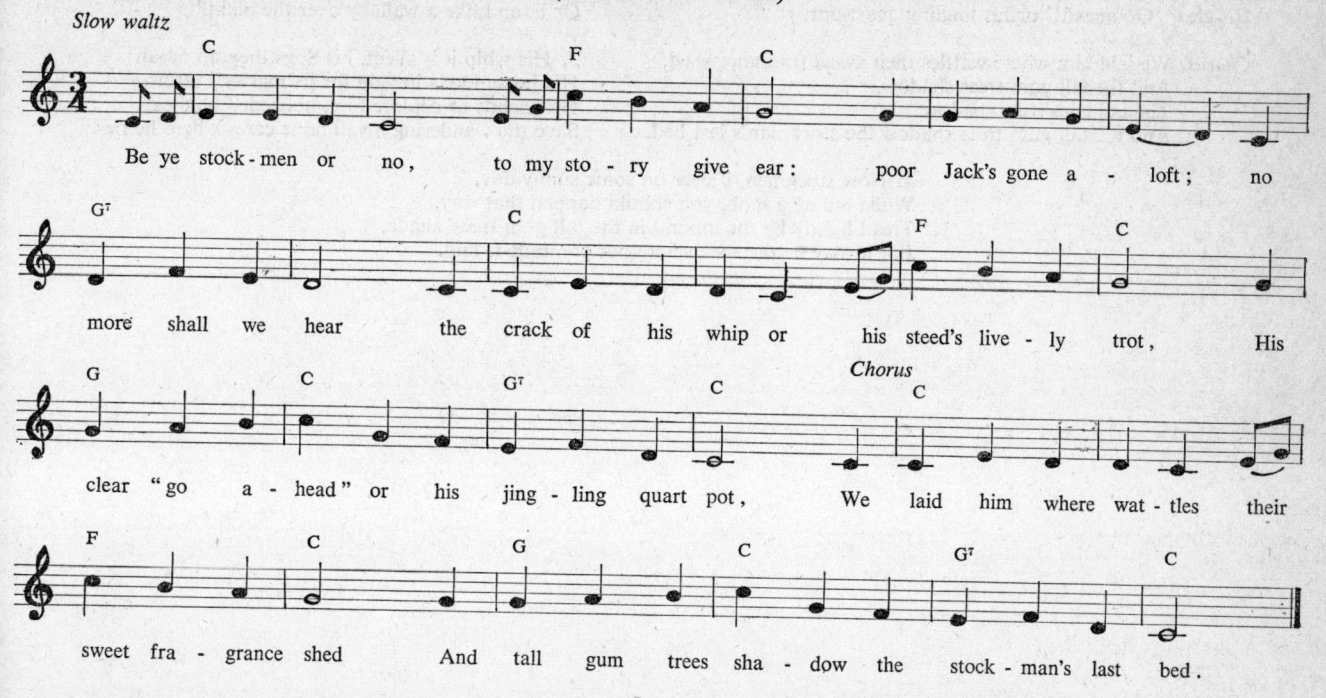

Slow waltz

Be ye stock-men or no, to my sto-ry give ear: poor Jack's gone a-loft; no more shall we hear the crack of his whip or his steed's live-ly trot, His clear "go a-head" or his jing-ling quart pot, *Chorus* We laid him where wat-tles their sweet fra-grance shed And tall gum trees sha-dow the stock-man's last bed.

1. Be ye stockmen or no, to my story give ear.
Poor Jack's gone aloft; no more shall we hear
The crack of his whip or his steed's lively trot,
His clear 'Go ahead!' or his jingling quart-pot.

Chorus: We laid him where wattles their sweet fragrance shed,
        And the tall gum trees shadow,
        The tall gum trees shadow,
        And the tall gum trees shadow the stockman's last bed.

2. While drafting one day he was horned by a cow.
'Alas!' cried poor Jack, 'it's all up with me now!
I ne'er shall be seen in the saddle again,
Or bound like a wallaby over the plain.'

3. His whip it is silent, his dogs they do moan;
His horse looks in vain for its master's return.
No friends to deplore him, unheeded he dies;
Save the wandering myall none cares where he lies.

4. Now stockmen, if ever on some sunny day,
While tailing a mob, you should happen that way,
Tread lightly by the mound in the tall gum trees' shade,
For it may be the spot where our comrade is laid.

THE OLD BARK HUT

Fairly quick

Oh, my name is Bob the swagman and I'll have you understand I've seen a lot of ups and downs while trav'ling thro' the land. I once was well to do, my lads, but now I'm so hard up That I'm forced to go on rations in an old bark hut.

Chorus
In an old bark hut In an old bark

hut. That I'm forced to go on ra-tions in an old bark hut.

(another version)

My name is Bob the swag-man and I'll have you un-der-stand I've seen a lot of ups and downs while trav'-ling thro' the land. I once was well to do, my lads, but now I'm so hard up That I'm forced to go on ra-tions in an old bark hut.

1. Oh, my name is Bob the Swagman, and I'll have you understand
I've seen a lot of ups and downs while travelling thro' the land;
I once was well to do, my lads, but now I'm so hard up
That I'm forced to go on rations in an old bark hut.

Chorus: In an old bark hut, in an old bark hut (*and repeat last line of verse*).

2. Ten pounds of flour, ten pounds of beef, some sugar and some tay,
That's all they give a hungry man until the seventh day.
If you don't be mighty sparing, you go with a hungry gut;
That's one of the great misfortunes of an old bark hut!

3. The bucket I wash me feet in has to cook me tay and stew;
They'd say I was getting mighty flash if I should ask for two.
The table's just a sheet of bark – God knows when it was cut!
It was blown from off the rafters of the old bark hut.

4. I've had the rain come pouring in just like a perfect flood,
Especially thro' the great big hole where once the table stood;
It leaves me not a single spot where I can lay me nut
But the rain is sure to find me in the old bark hut.

5. Beside the fire I lay me down, wrapped up in two old rugs;
You couldn't call it comfort, but it seems to lure the bugs!
And all I've got for company's the poor old collie slut,
So I use her for a pillow in the old bark hut.

6. So now I've sung my little song as nicely as I could;
I hope the ladies present will not think my language rude.
And all you handsome girls and boys, around me growing up,
Remember Bob the Swagman in his old bark hut.

THE STATION COOK

The song I'm going to sing to you will not de-tain you long, It is all a-bout a sta-tion cook we had at Old Pin-yong. His pas-try was so beauti-ful, his cook-ing was so fine, That it gave us all the sto-mach ache all thro' the shear-ing time.

1. The song I'm going to sing to you will not detain you long,
It is all about a station cook we had at old Pinyong.
His pastry was so beautiful, his cooking was so fine,
That it gave us all a stomach-ache right through the shearing time.

2. Oh, you should see his plum-duffs, his doughboys and his pies,
I swear by Long Maloney they'd open a shearer's eyes.
He'd say, 'Take your time, good fellows,' and he'd fix us with a glance,
Saying, 'I'll dish you up much better, if you'll give me half a chance.'

3. Oh, you should see his doughboys, his dumplings and his pies,
The thought of such luxuries would open a shearer's eyes.
He gets up in the morning, gives us plenty of stewed tea,
And don't forget, when shearing's done, to sling the cook his fee.

4. But, oh dear! I feel so queer, I don't know what to do,
The thought of leaving Fowler's Bay just breaks my heart in two.
But if ever I catch that slushy I'll make him rue the day
That he ruined my constitution while shearing at Fowler's Bay.

OLD BLACK ALICE

Brisk

Old Black A-lice are my name Well-shot are my sta-tion, It's no dis-grace, the old black face it's the co-lour of my na-tion, Bin-di-eye-eye and mind your eye and don't kick up a shin-dy. I've got a boy in Ca-moo-weal and one in Goon-di-win-di.

1. Old Black Alice are my name, Wellshot are my station;
It's no disgrace, the old black face, it's the colour of my nation.
Bindieye-eye and mind your eye, and don't kick up a shindy;
I've got a boy in Camooweal, and one in Goondiwindi.

2. I can polka, I can waltz, I can dance the figures;
White man find 'em too much work, teach 'em to the niggers!
Dance me up and dance me down, I don't mind your colour,
I've got a boy in Kingaroy and one in Cunnamulla.

3. God He made the lubra girl that all the white girls run down;
He made the whites by light of day, the black ones after sundown.
Dance the black girl round and round, don't you dare despise her!
I've got a man at Cuddapan, and another one at Mount Isa.

4. White man wash in old tin tub, black man wash much cleaner;
Black man wash in Condamine and in the Di'mantina.
Listen to the beat and mind your feet; don't exhaust my patience!
I'm off next week to Combo Creek to meet my fine relations.

JACKY-JACKY

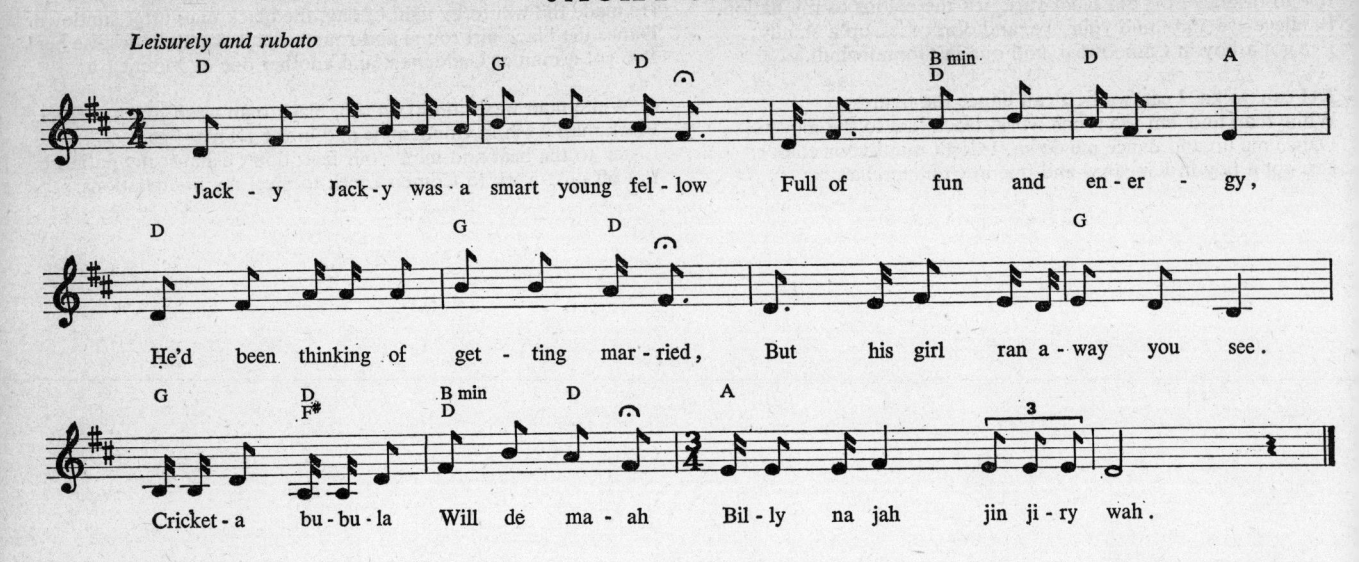

Leisurely and rubato

Jack-y Jack-y was a smart young fel-low Full of fun and en-er-gy,

He'd been thinking of get-ting mar-ried, But his girl ran a-way you see.

Cricket-a bu-bu-la Will de ma-ah Bil-ly na jah jin ji-ry wah.

1. Jacky-Jacky was a smart young fellow,
    Full of fun and energy;
 He'd been thinking of getting married,
    But his girl ran away, you see.

Chorus: Cricketa bubula will de ma-ah,
            Billy na jah jin ji-ry wah.

2. Jacky-Jacky used to chase the emus
    With his spear and waddy too.
 He's the only man that can tell you
    What the emu told the kangaroo.

3. The hunting days was Jacky's business
    Till the white man came along,
 Put his fences across the country;
    Now the hunting days are gone.

4. White fellow wants to pay all taxes,
    Keep Jacky-Jacky in clothes and food;
 Jacky doesn't care what becomes of the country –
    White fellow tucker him very good!

5. Now the country's short of money,
    Jacky-Jacky sits and he laughs all day;
 White fellow wants to give it back to Jacky –
    No fear! Jacky won't have it that way!

FIVE AND A ZACK

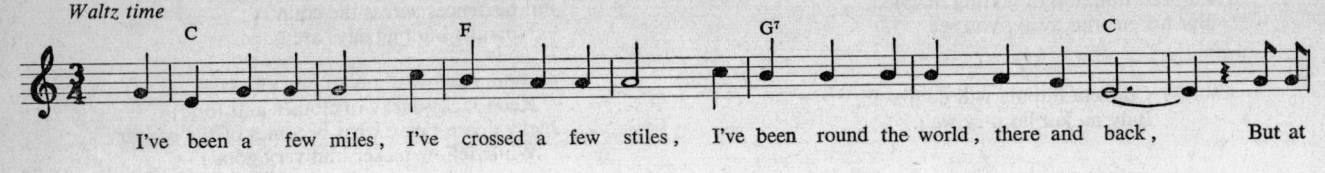

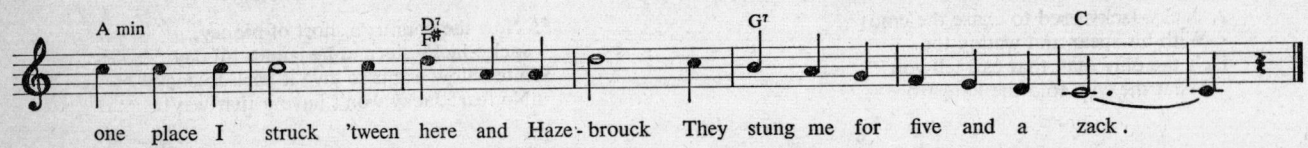

Waltz time

I've been a few miles, I've crossed a few stiles, I've been round the world, there and back, But at one place I struck 'tween here and Haze-brouck They stung me for five and a zack.

1. I've been a few miles, I've crossed a few stiles,
   I've been round the world, there and back;
   But at one place I struck, 'tween here and Hazebrouck,
   They stung me for five and a zack.

2. The timekeeper there, with his sanctified air,
   Is a Salvation Army lance-jack;
   On his cornet he'll bleat when they play in the street,
   But he stung me for five and a zack.

3. The job's at an end; I'm camped in the bend,
   And I hate the whole duck-shoving pack.
   It's not that I'm broke or in need of a smoke,
   But they stung me for five and a zack.

4. May that time-keeper stand in an Aunt Sally band,
   And blow till his eyeballs turn black!
   May each note of his cornet turn into a hornet,
   And sting him for five and a zack.

5. When my time comes, I'll go to the hot place below,
   And I never intend to come back.
   On my tombstone you'll find these words underlined:
   'They stung me for five and a zack.'

THE RAM OF DALBY

1. As I went to Dalby, upon a market day,
I saw the finest sheep there was ever fed on hay.

Chorus: Aye wrinkle darby, darby wrinkle day,
Wrinkle wrinkle darby, for darby can today.

2. The wool grew on his belly, it grew into the ground;
Cut off and sent to Dalby, it fetched a thousand pound.

3. The wool grew on his backbone, the wool grew up so high
A hawk had built her nest there, I heard the young ones cry.

4. The wool grew on his shoulders, it grew up to the moon;
A man went up in September, and never came down till June.

5. The man who raised this sheep up, he must be mighty rich;
The man who made this song up is a lying son of the West!

EUABALONG BALL

Quick waltz

Oh who has-n't heard of Eu - a - ba - long Ball where the lads of the Lach - lan the great and the small Come bent on di - ver - sion from far and from near To shake off their trou - bles for just once a year.

1. Oh who hasn't heard of Euabalong Ball,
Where the lads of the Lachlan, the great and the small,
Come bent on diversion from far and from near
To shake off their troubles for just once a year?

2. There were sheilas in plenty, some two or three score,
Some weaners, some two-tooths and some rather more;
With their fleeces all scoured so fluffy and clean,
The finest young sheilas there ever were seen.

3. The music struck up, and it set us a pace!
Some danced at a canter, and some tried to race,
And I soon heard the manager let out a curse
As somebody caught him a dig with their spurs.

4. The bounday riders went bounding about,
But the well-sinkers seemed to be feeling the drought;
Tho' the water was scarce, there was whiskey to spare –
What they couldn't swallow they rubbed in their hair!

5. Euabalong Ball was a wonderful sight:
The rams danced the two-tooths the whole flaming night!
And many's the man who may blush to recall
The polkas he danced at Euabalong Ball.

THE STRINGYBARK COCKATOO

Marching pace

I'm a broke alluvial miner who's been used his cup to drain, And it's many a time it caused me for to lie in frost and rain. Roaming round about the country looking for some work to do, Oh I started a job of reaping for a stringybark cockatoo.

Chorus

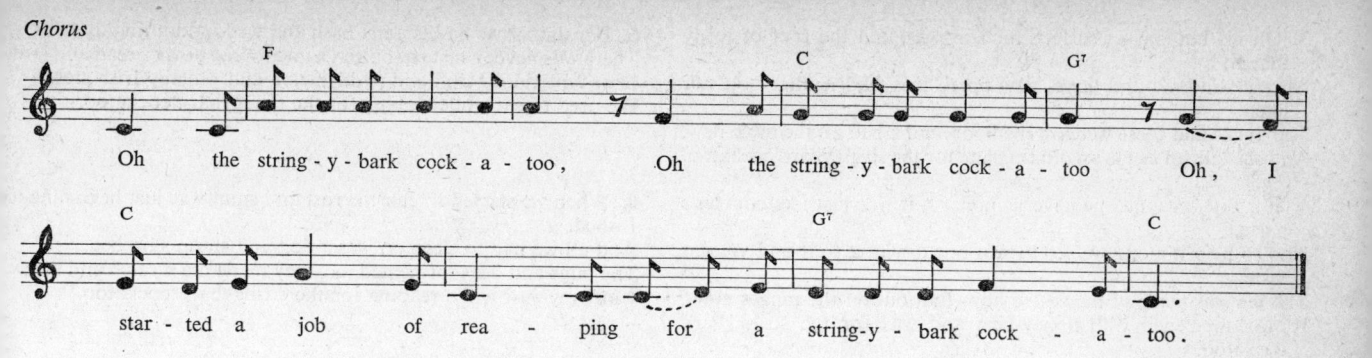

Oh the string-y-bark cock-a-too, Oh the string-y-bark cock-a-too Oh, I started a job of rea - ping for a string-y-bark cock - a - too.

1. I'm a broke alluvial miner who's been used his cup to drain,
And it's many a time it caused me for to lie in frost and rain.
Roaming round about the country looking for some work to do,
Oh, I started a job of reaping for a stringybark cockatoo.

Chorus: Oh, the stringybark cockatoo,
Oh, the stringybark cockatoo,
Oh, I started a job of reaping for a stringybark cockatoo!

2. Ten shillings an acre was his price, with promise of fairish board,
And he said that his crops were very light, 'twas all he could afford.
He drove me out in a bullock dray and the piggery met my view,
But the pigs and the sheep were in the wheat of the stringybark cockatoo.

Chorus: (*as before, repeating last line of verse just sung.*)

3. Oh his hut was of surface mud, it was, and the roof of reedy thatch;
All the windows and doors flew open, they had neither bolt nor latch.
The ducks and geese were on the floor, and a hen on the table flew,
And she laid an egg in an old tin plate for the stringybark cockatoo.

4. For our breakfast he gave us pollard, it was just like cobbler's paste,
And to help it along we got brown bread with a sour and vinegar taste.
The tea was made of the native hops that out on the ranges grew;
It was sweetened with honey-bees and wax for the stringybark cockatoo.

5. For dinner we had goanna hash and we found it mighty hard.
There was never a taste of butter, so we forced down bread and lard.
It was quondong duff and paddymelon and wallaby Irish stew
We used to eat while reaping for the stringybark cockatoo.

6. When we started to cut, the rust and smut was just beginning to shed,
And all we had to sleep on was a dog-and-sheep-skin bed.
The bugs and fleas tormented me, they made me scratch and screw.
I lost my rest while reaping for the stringybark cockatoo.

7. At night when the work was over then I'd nurse the youngest child,
And whenever I said a joking word the mother would laugh and smile.
The cocky he grew jealous, and he thumped me black and blue,
And he drove me away without a rap, did the stringybark cockatoo.

OH, GIVE ME A HUT
(The Free-Selector)

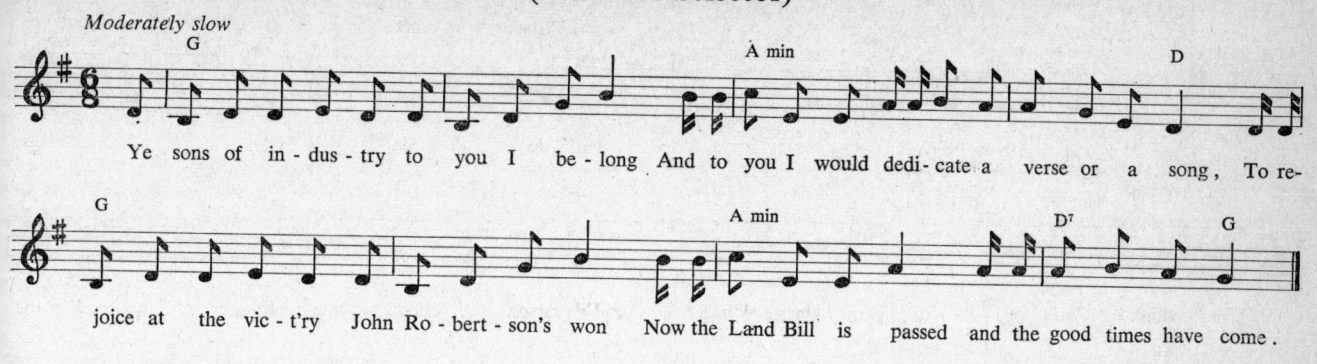

1. Ye sons of industry, to you I belong,
And to you I would dedicate a verse or a song
To rejoice at the victory John Robertson's won,
Now the Land Bill is passed and the good times have come.

Chorus: Then give me a hut in my own native land,
   Or a tent in Australia where the tall gum trees stand;
   No matter how far in the bush it may be,
   If the dear native girl will but share it with me.

2. No more with our swags through the bush need we roam
Imploring of charity to give us a home,
For the land is unfettered, and we may reside
In a home of our own by some clear waterside.

3. We will plant our own garden and sow our own field,
And eat of the fruits which industry will yield,
And be independent, as long we have strived,
Tho' those who have ruled us the right long denied.

THE COCKIES OF BUNGAREE

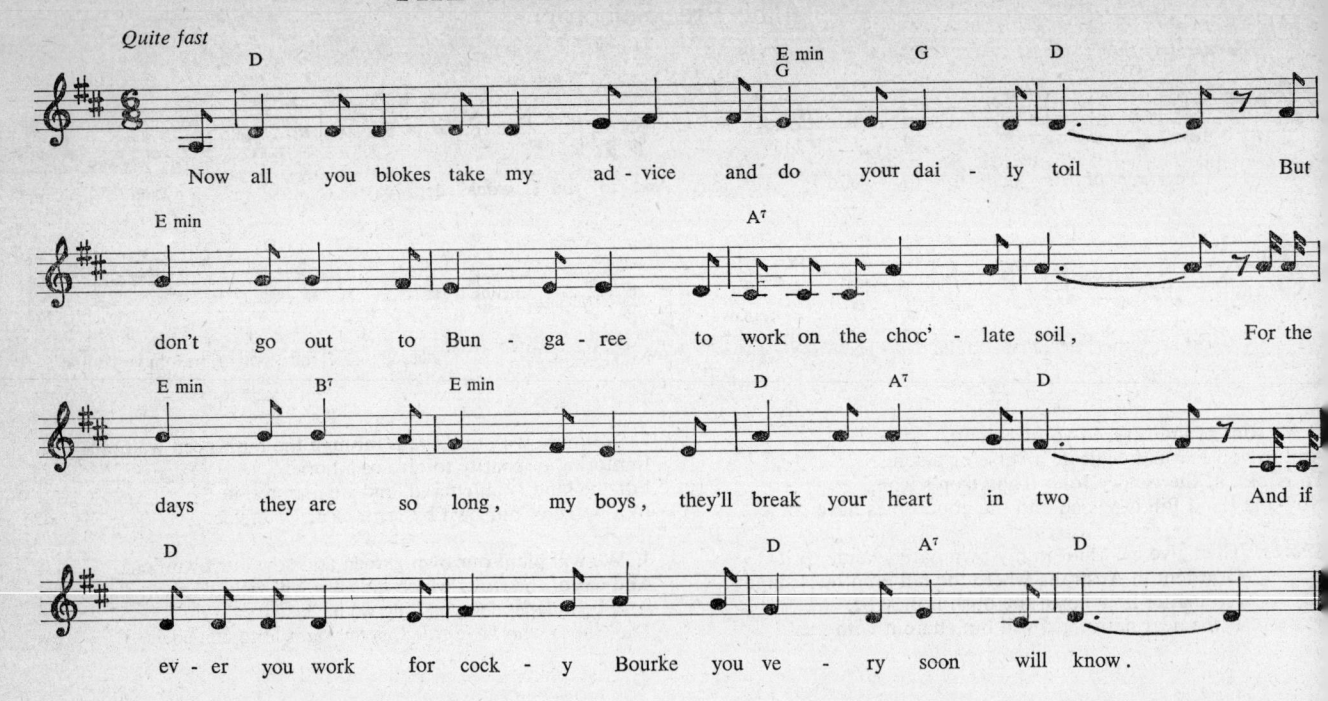

Quite fast

Now all you blokes take my ad-vice and do your dai-ly toil, But don't go out to Bun-ga-ree to work on the choc'-late soil, For the days they are so long, my boys, they'll break your heart in two And if ev-er you work for cock-y Bourke you ve-ry soon will know.

1. Now, all you blokes, take my advice and do your daily toil,
But don't go out to Bungaree to work on the chocolate soil.
For the days they are so long, my boys, they'll break your heart in two;
And if ever you work for cocky Bourke you very soon will know.

Chorus: Oh we used to go to bed, you know, a little bit after dark.
　　　　 The room we used to sleep in, it was just like Noah's Ark:
　　　　 There were dogs and rats and mice and cats and pigs and poulteree.
　　　　 I'll never forget the time we had while down in Bungaree!

2. On the thirsty Monday morning, sure, to work I had to go.
My noble cocky says to me, 'Get up! You're rather slow.'
The moon was shining gloriously, and the stars were out, you see,
And I thought before the sun would rise I'ld die in Bungaree.

3. Oh, he called me to my supper at half past eight or nine,
He called me to my breakfast before the sun could shine,
And after tea was over, all with a merry laugh,
The — old cocky says to me, 'We'll cut a bit of chaff.'

4. 'Now when you are chaff-cutting, boys, isn't it a spell?'
'Yes, be Jove,' says I, 'it is, and it's me that knows it well!'
For many of those fellows with me they disagree,
For I hate the jolly nightwork that they do in Bungaree.

EUMERELLA SHORE

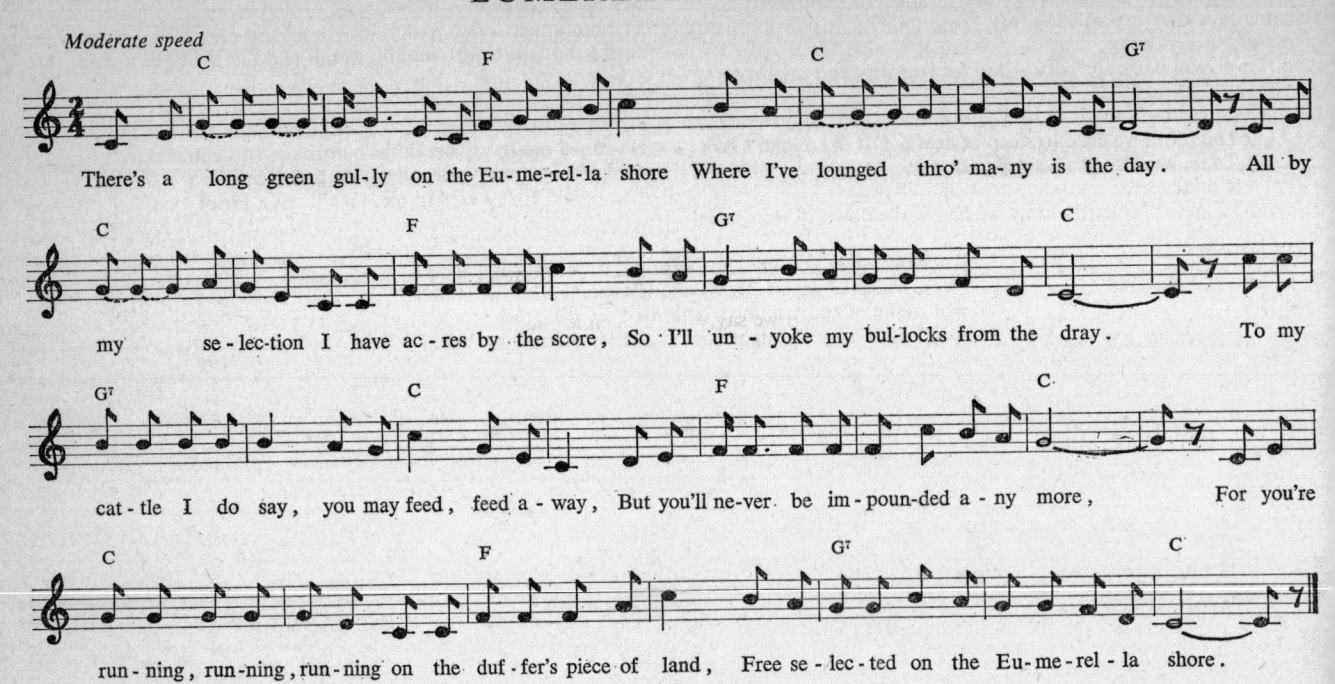

Moderate speed

There's a long green gul-ly on the Eu-me-rel-la shore Where I've lounged thro' ma-ny is the day. All by my se-lec-tion I have ac-res by the score, So I'll un-yoke my bul-locks from the dray. To my cat-tle I do say, you may feed, feed a-way, But you'll ne-ver be im-poun-ded a-ny more, For you're run-ning, run-ning, run-ning on the duf-fer's piece of land, Free se-lec-ted on the Eu-me-rel-la shore.

1. There's a long green gully on the Eumerella Shore,
Where I've lounged through many is the day.
All by my selection I have acres by the score
So I'll unyoke my bullocks from the dray.
To my cattle I do say, you may feed, feed away,
But you'll never be impounded any more,
For you're running, running, running on the duffer's piece of land
Free selected on the Eumerella Shore.

2. When the moon is shining bright and has climbed the mountains high
We will saddle up our horses and away.
We will steal the squatter's cattle by the darkness of the night,
And we'll brand at the dawn of the day.
And now my pretty calf at the squatter you may laugh,
But you'll never see your owner any more.
For you're running, running, running on the duffer's piece of land
Free selected on the Eumerella Shore.

3. And when we get the swag, we'll steal the squatter's nag,
And we'll sell him in some distant inland town,
And when we get the cash, oh, we chaps will cut a dash
For the doing of the squatter so brown.
To John Robertson we say, you've been leading us astray,
And we never can believe you any more;
For we chaps can get a livin' far easier by thievin'
Than by farming on the Eumerella Shore.

THE LIMEJUICE TUB
(The Whalers' Rhyme)

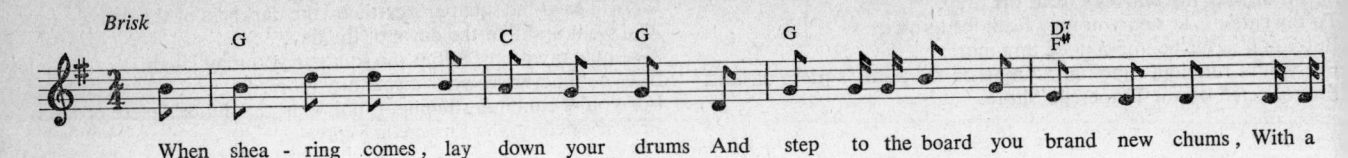

Lyrics under music: When shea-ring comes, lay down your drums And step to the board you brand new chums, With a rah-dum, rah-dum rub-a-dub dub We'll send you back to the lime-juice tub.

1. When shearing comes, lay down your drums,
And step to the board, you brand-new-chums.
With a rah-dum, rah-dum, rub-a-dub-dub,
We'll send you back to the limejuice tub.

2. The brand-new-chums and cockies' sons
All fancy that they are great guns,
They fancy they can shear the wool,
But the beggars can only tear and pull.

3. They tar the sheep till they're nearly black –
Roll up, roll up, and get the sack! –
Then press the wool without any bales;
Oh, shearing's hell in New South Wales.

4. You cockatoos, you never need fret!
To show you up I'll not forget.
For I'm the man that's ready to bet
You're over your heels, head first in debt.

5. Although you live beyond your means,
Your daughters wear no crinolines,
Nor are they troubled with boots or shoes,
For they're wild in the bush with the kangaroos.

6. At home, at home I'd like to be,
Not humping my drum in the back countree;
Sixteen thousand miles I've come
To march along with my blanket drum.

THE INGLEWOOD COCKY
(*or*, The New England Cocky)

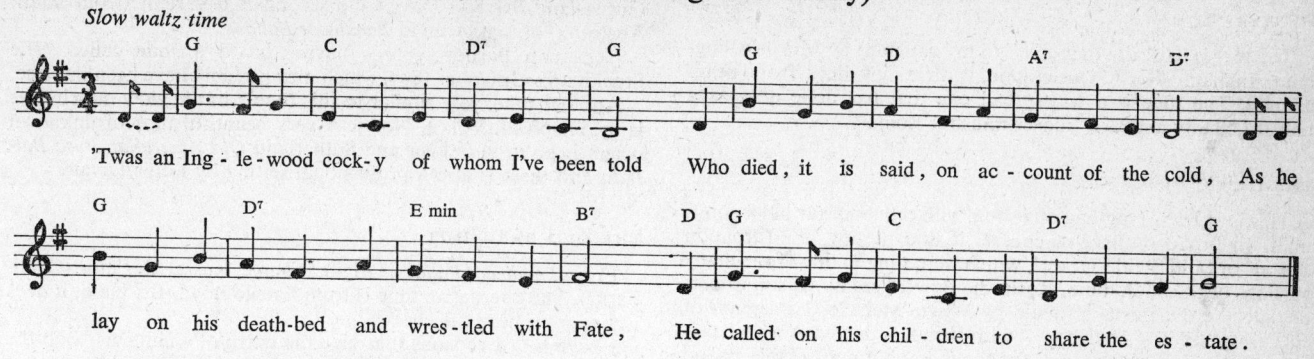

1. 'Twas an Inglewood cocky of whom I've been told
Who died, it is said, on account of the cold.
As he lay on his deathbed and wrestled with Fate,
He called on his children to share the estate.

2. 'Let John have the pig and the pet native bear,
The old kangaroo can be Margaret's share;
Let Mike have the possum that comes when he's called,
And Katy the emu although he's gone bald.

3. 'To Mary I'm leaving the pink cockatoo,
And that's about all your poor father can do.
There's fish in the creek and there's fowl on the lake;
Let each take as much as they're able to take.

4. 'Farewell, my dear children, no more can I leave.
Don't quarrel, or else my poor spirit will grieve.
And if you should marry, and have children to rear,
Remember I nursed you on pumpkin and beer.'

NOTES

MUSTERING DAY

The text is basically that given to my daughter by Mrs J. Allingham, Ingham, North Queensland, with a few lines from other sources. The tune is a widespread one that has done duty as a halyard chanty and as a 'nigger-minstrel' song.

THE DYING STOCKMAN

This is a strange rag-bag of a song, with echoes of far older songs in it. In broad outline, of course, it is a parody of 'Tarpaulin Jacket' or 'Old Stable Jacket', which were sung to one of the many versions of the fiddle-tune 'Rosin the Bow'. I see no reason to perpetuate the old mistake (made by Whyte-Melville, I imagine) of confusing 'bow' – fiddlebow – with 'beau' – dandy. Another version of the same tune is used for the funny but unprintable ballad 'Lady Monroe'.

The verses and tune given here are from *Singabout*, Vol. 3, No. 1, taken down from the singing of Mrs Laver, Mosman, daughter of Lance Skuthorpe. The notes I have marked with an asterisk are prolonged by other singers to a length of five crotchets. The more familiar tune is also printed.

THE STOCKMAN'S LAST BED

The text was among the first bush songs to be printed. It is distinctly 'jackaroo' in feeling. Anderson says that it was written to the Dibdin tune 'The Boatswain's Last Whistle', but this does not fit it particularly well. Of the two tunes given here, the first is from the *Queensland Pocket Songbook*, learnt as a child in Maryborough, Queensland, by Syd Davis; the second is a variant (from South Australia) of that given in *Bandicoot Ballads*.

Nehemiah Bartley records having heard a song called 'The Stockman's Grave' in 1857, which may possibly have been this one.

Another tune, very similar to this tune 2 but in slow march time is in *Singabout*, Vol. 4, No. 3. A very beautiful tune of unknown origin is given in Palmer and Sutherland *Old Australian Bush Ballads*, and there is also a professional setting by Louis Lavater.

THE OLD BARK HUT

From *Bandicoot Ballads*. Original source, Russel Singleton ('Ironbark'). The alternative tune is from Estelle Boyd, Brisbane; it does not seem to have the chorus.

I have heard versions that give the narrator's name as 'Bob the Cracksman' or 'Bob the Magsman', thus pointing back to convict origins. Other tunes (both oddly enough without chorus) are in the *Overlander Songbook* and in Anderson's *Colonial Ballads*.

THE STATION COOK

Collected by Dr Percy Jones, Melbourne. Tune from *Singabout*, Vol. 2, No. 2.

OLD BLACK ALICE

From the *Queensland Pocket Songbook*: tune from Bill Scott, harmonization by the late Dr Dalley-Scarlett, text composite from several sources.

JACKY-JACKY

Recorded from the singing of Herb and Fred Walker, Tongala, Victoria, by the Folklore Society of Victoria. Additional verses are from Jim Adams, formerly of Barmah.

Singabout, Vol. 4, No. 1, prints a different version, more regular in its barring.

FIVE AND A ZACK

From the singing of Keith Waller, North Stradbroke Island, Moreton Bay. He learnt it in the 1920s in the Murrumbidgee Irrigation Area. 'Zack' is still current slang for 'sixpence'.

THE RAM OF DALBY

From the *Queensland Pocket Songbook*. English origin, with words altered by the swingover from mutton to wool.

EUABALONG BALL

Learnt from Australian students abroad, *circa* 1935. The text given by Stewart and Keesing as 'The Wooyeo Ball' seems to have passed through more proletarian hands than those of 'Vox Silvis' named there as the author. A longer version has been collected by the Queensland Folklore Society.

THE STRINGYBARK COCKATOO

Another song of Mr Ames, completed by the addition of some verses from Paterson. Mrs Penberthy, from Cairns but now of Brisbane, tells me that her family sang these verses to the tune of 'A Life on the Ocean Wave'. Anderson gives the tune 'Little Polly Perkins' but without indication of how to fit the words to it.

OH, GIVE ME A HUT (THE FREE-SELECTOR)

Composite. The text is from Paterson, the tune from the *Queensland Pocket Songbook*, where it is used for 'Oh, Give Me a Hut'. This latter set of words also appears at full length in Stewart and Keesing. Jack Bradshaw has a fanciful story that Ned Kelly used to ask his sister Kate to sing this song to him, and records a variant line of the chorus:

'If a girl like Kate Kelly would share it with me'.

I have been told that the same tune is used for a local ballad in Buckinghamshire, England. There is quite a different tune in Palmer and Sutherland, *Old Australian Bush Ballads*.

THE COCKIES OF BUNGAREE

Recorded from the singing of Simon McDonald, Creswick, Victoria, by the Folklore Society of Victoria. Mr McDonald repeats the chorus at irregular intervals: but it seems the song could be treated as a solo, using the chorus simply as an additional verse after verse 1.

EUMERELLA SHORE

I rather hold to the idea that this is a squatter song satirizing free-selection; not a genuine free-selector song. Most of the free-selectors were a painfully respectable and law-abiding lot, and would hardly sing of the delights of poddy-dodging.

There is some dispute about the actual geographical locale of the song. There is a Eumerella river in Victoria, reaching the sea between Portland and Port Fairy; and there is a Umerella or Numerella river in New South Wales that joins the Upper Murrumbidgee just north of Cooma. The reference to (Sir) John Robertson appears to favour New South Wales. According to Anderson, the text was printed in 1861 in *The Launceston Examiner*.

According to *Singabout*, Vol. 2, No. 2, from which this is taken the tune comes from the same stock as 'Maggie May' by way of a drawing-room version called 'Nellie Gray'. Many slight variants are known, and there is a setting by Louis Lavater.

THE LIMEJUICE TUB (THE WHALERS' RHYME)

This came mainly from the singing of Bill Scott, with a few additional lines from Stewart and Keesing. Anderson prints the tune in 6/8 time and gives its title as 'Paddy's Land'.

THE INGLEWOOD COCKY (*or* The New England Cocky)

This was given to me by Mr P. Ames at Kyabram, Victoria. It is very close to 'The New England Cocky', printed by Paterson, but I think it is tauter and funnier. I imagine that I detect an echo of 'The Roast Beef of Old England' in the tune; this sort of subconscious pun sometimes gives a link between an old tune and its new words.

5
THE NOMADS

DROVERS, shearers, sheepwashers, bullockies, cane-cutters and other tradesmen travel in the way of business. Swagmen, the station-hands used to say, travel out of the way of business. The generalization is unjust, as there are all kinds of swagmen, from the cove genuinely in search of work to the rare incendiary maniac.

All the same, there is a distinction between the tradesmen's songs, bursting with vigour and solidarity, and the swagman songs dripping with romantic self-pity. Railwaymen's songs, sung on long lonely journeys, are the only ones to equal the swagman songs in this respect. There are joyful exceptions, but not very many.

Drover songs fall into two groups: long ballads normally without a chorus sung to quieten nervous cattle at night; and chorus-songs asserting the superiority of drovers, particularly the Queensland overlanders, to the rest of creation. These latter are sung after a successful trip rather than during it.

Shearers have their boasting-songs too, for individual 'guns' or 'ringers'; but they also have satiric songs that make fun of the boasters. The other shearer-speciality is songs on the early battles of Unionism; but not many of these have come down to us in their sung form.

A distinct influence of current American 'minstrel' and plantation songs is apparent in some of the tunes here.

The notes to each song in this part are on page 148 of this book.

THE QUEENSLAND DROVER
(The Overlander)

Fast

There's a trade you all know well, It's bring-ing cat-tle o-ver On ev'-ry track to the gulf and back men know the Queens-land dro-ver. Pass the bil-ly round, my boys! Don't let the pint-pot stand there, For to-night we drink the health of ev'-ry O-ver-lan-der.

THE QUEENSLAND DROVER
(another version)

There's a trade you all know well, It's bringing cattle over On ev'—ry track to the gulf and back men know the Queensland drover.

Chorus

Pass the billy round, my boys! Don't let the pint-pot stand there, For tonight we drink the health of ev'ry O—ver-lander.

1. There's a trade you all know well,
    It's bringing cattle over.
 On every track, to the Gulf and back,
    Men know the Queensland drover.

Chorus: Pass the billy round, my boys!
             Don't let the pint-pot stand there!
         For tonight we drink the health
             Of every overlander.

2. I come from the Northern plains
    Where the girls and grass are scanty;
 Where the creeks run dry or ten foot high
    And it's either drought or plenty.

3. There are men from every land,
    From Spain and France and Flanders;
 They're a well-mixed pack, both white and black,
    The Queensland overlanders.

4. When we've earned a spree in town
    We live like pigs in clover;
 And the whole year's cheque pours down the neck
    Of many a Queensland drover.

5. As I pass along the roads,
    The children raise my dander
 Crying 'Mother dear, take in the clothes,
    Here comes an overlander!'

6. Now I'm bound for home once more,
    On a prad that's quite a goer;
 I can find a job with a crawling mob
    On the banks of the Maranoa.

THE UNION BOY

When I first arrived in Quirindi, those girls they jumped with joy, Saying one unto the other "Here comes a Union boy".

1. When I first arrived in Quirindi, those girls they jumped with joy,
   Saying one unto the other, 'Here comes a union boy!

2. 'We'll treat him to a bottle, and likewise to a dram,
   Our hearts we'll freely give, too, to all staunch union men.'

3. I had not long been in Quirindi, not one week, two, or three,
   When a handsome pretty fair maid she fell in love with me.

4. She introduced me to her mother as a loyal union man,
   'Oh mother, dearest mother, now he's gently joined the gang!'

5. 'Oh daughter, dearest daughter, oh this can never be,
   For four years ago-oh he scabbed it at Forquadee.'

6. 'Oh mother, dearest mother, now the truth to you I'll tell,
   He's since then joined the union, and the country knows it well.'

7. 'Now Fred, you've joined the union, so stick to it like glue,
   For the scabs that were upon your back, they're now but only few.

8. 'And if ever you go blacklegging or scabbing it likewise,
   It's with my long, long fingernails I'll scratch out both your eyes.'

9. 'I'll put you to every cruelty, I'll stretch you in a vice,
   I'll cut you up in a hay machine and sell you for Chinee rice.'

10. Come all you young and old men, oh, wherever you may be,
    Oh it's hoist-oh the flag-oh, the flag of unity!

11. Then scabbing in this country will soon be at an end,
    And I pray that one and all of you will be staunch union men.

THE RYEBUCK SHEARER

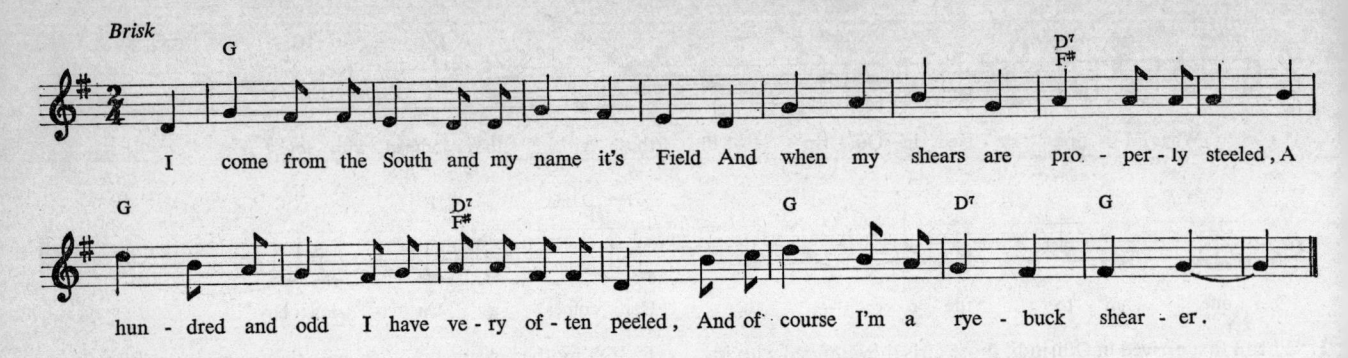

1. I come from the South and my name it's Field,
   And when my shears are properly steeled,
   A hundred and odd I have very often peeled,
   And of course I'm a ryebuck shearer.

   Chorus: If I don't shear a tally before I go,
   My shears and stone in the river I'll throw.
   I'll never open Sawbees to take another blow
   And prove I'm a ryebuck shearer.

2. There's a bloke on the board and I heard him say
That I couldn't shear a hundred sheep a day,
But some fine day I'll show him the way,
And prove I'm a ryebuck shearer.

3. Oh, I'll make a splash, but I won't say when,
I'll hop off me tail and I'll into the pen,
While the ringer's shearing five, I'll shear ten,
And prove I'm a ryebuck shearer.

4. There's a bloke on the board and he's got a yellow skin,
A very long nose and he shaves on the chin,
And a voice like a billy-goat dancing on a tin,
And of course he's a ryebuck shearer.

LADIES OF BRISBANE
(The Drover's Song)

Tune: "Spanish Ladies"

Farewell and adieu to you Brisbane Ladies, farewell and adieu to the girls of Toowong: We have sold all our cattle and cannot now linger, But we hope we shall see you again before long.

Repeat for Chorus

1. Farewell and adieu to you Brisbane ladies,
   Farewell and adieu to the girls of Toowong;
We have sold all our cattle and cannot now linger,
   But we hope we shall see you again before long.

Chorus: For we rant and we roar like true Queensland natives,
   We rant and we roar as onward we push,
Until we return to the 'old cattle station'
   What joy and delight is the life in the bush!

2. The first camp we make is called the Quart-pot,
   Caboolture and Kilcoy, then Colinton hut;
We pull up at Stonehouse, Bob Williams' paddock,
   And early next morning we cross the Blackbutt.

3. On, on! past Taromeo to Yarraman Creek, boys!
   It's there where we'll make a fine camp for the day,
Where the water and grass are both plenty and good, boys.
   The life of a drover is merry and gay.

4. Now the camp is all snug and supper is over,
   We sit round the fire enjoying a smoke
And yarning of dogs and of cattle and horses
   Till all join in chorus to 'Grandfather's Clock'.

5. Then it's right through Nanango, that jolly old township,
   'Good day to you, lads' with a hearty shake-hands;
'Come on, this is my shout!' 'Well, here's to our next trip,
   And we hope you'll come back, boys, tonight to our dance.'

6. Oh, the girls look so pretty; the sight is entrancing;
   Bewitching and graceful they join in the fun,
The waltz, polka, first step and all other dancing
   To the old concertina of Jack Smith the Don.

7. Now fill up your glasses and drink to our lasses;
   Come, sing the loud chorus, sing farewell to all.
Until we return to the 'old cattle station',
   We'll always be pleased to give you a call.

LADIES OF BRISBANE
(Augathella Station)

Fare-well and a-dieu to you sweet Bris-bane La-dies, Fare-well and a-dieu to you girls of Too-wong, For we've sold all our cat-tle and have to be mo-ving, But we hope we shall see you a-gain be-fore long.

Repeat for Chorus

1. Farewell and adieu to you, sweet Brisbane ladies,
Farewell and adieu to you girls of Toowong,
For we've sold all our cattle, and have to be moving,
But we hope we shall see you again before long.

Chorus: We'll rant and we'll roar like true Queensland drovers,
We'll rant and we'll roar as onwards we push,
Until we get back to the Augathella Station,
For it's flaming dry going through the old Queensland bush.

2. The first camp we make, we shall call it the Quart-pot,
Caboolture, then Kilcoy and Colinton's Hut;
We'll pull up at the Stone House, Bob Williamson's paddock,
And early next morning we cross the Blackbutt.

3. Then on to Taromeo and Yarraman Creek, lads,
It's there we shall make our next camp for the day,
Where the water and grass are both plenty and sweet, lads,
And maybe we'll butcher a fat little stray.

4. Then on to Nanango, that hardbitten township,
Where the out-of-work station hands sit in the dust,
And the shearers get shorn by old Tim the contractor –
Oh I wouldn't go near there but I flaming well must!

5. The girls of Toomancey they look so entrancing,
Those young bawling heifers are out for their fun!
With the waltz and the polka and all kinds of dancing,
To the racketty old banjo of Bob Anderson.

6. Then fill up your glasses and drink to the lasses;
We'll drink this town dry, then farewell to them all;
And when we've got back to the Augathella Station
We'll hope you come by there and pay us a call.

7. We'll rant and we'll roar like true Queensland drovers,
We'll rant and we'll roar as onward we push,
Until we get back to the Augathella Station,
For its flaming dry going through the old Queensland bush.

THE DROVER'S DREAM

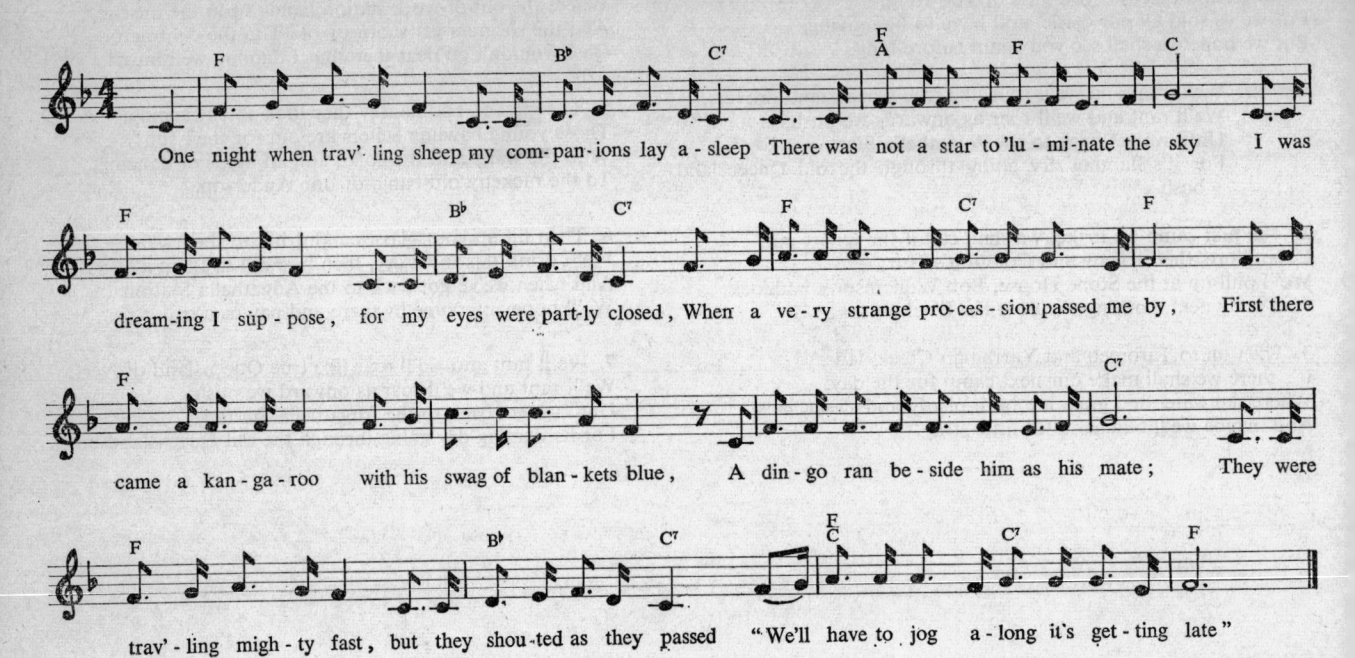

One night when trav'ling sheep my companions lay asleep There was not a star to 'luminate the sky I was dreaming I suppose, for my eyes were partly closed, When a very strange procession passed me by, First there came a kangaroo with his swag of blankets blue, A dingo ran beside him as his mate; They were trav'ling mighty fast, but they shouted as they passed "We'll have to jog along it's getting late"

1. One night when travelling sheep, my companions lay asleep,
There was not a star to 'luminate the sky,
I was dreaming I suppose, for my eyes were partly closed,
When a very strange procession passed me by.
First there came a kangaroo with his swag of blankets blue,
A dingo ran beside him as his mate;
They were travelling mighty fast, but they shouted as they passed,
'We'll have to jog along, it's getting late!'

2. The pelican and the crane they came in from off the plain
To amuse the company with a Highland Fling;
The dear old bandicoot played the tune upon his flute,
And the native bears sat round them in a ring.
The drongo and the crow sang us songs of long ago,
The frill-necked lizard listened with a smile,
And the emu standing near with his claw up to his ear
Said: 'Funniest thing I've heard for quite a while!'

3. The frogs from out the swamp where the atmosphere is damp
Came bounding in and sat upon the stones.
They each unrolled their swags, and produced from little bags
The violin, the banjo and the bones.
The goanna and the snake and the adder wide awake
With an alligator danced The Soldier's Joy.
In the spreading silky-oak the jackass cracked a joke,
And the magpie sang The Wild Colonial Boy.

4. Some brolgas darted out from the tea-tree all about,
And performed a set of Lancers very well.
Then the parrot green and blue gave the orchestra its cue
To strike up The Old Log Cabin in the Dell.
I was dreaming I suppose, of these entertaining shows,
But it never crossed my mind I was asleep,
Till the boss beneath the cart woke me up with such a start
Yelling: 'Dreamy, where the hell are all the sheep?'

GOORIANAWA

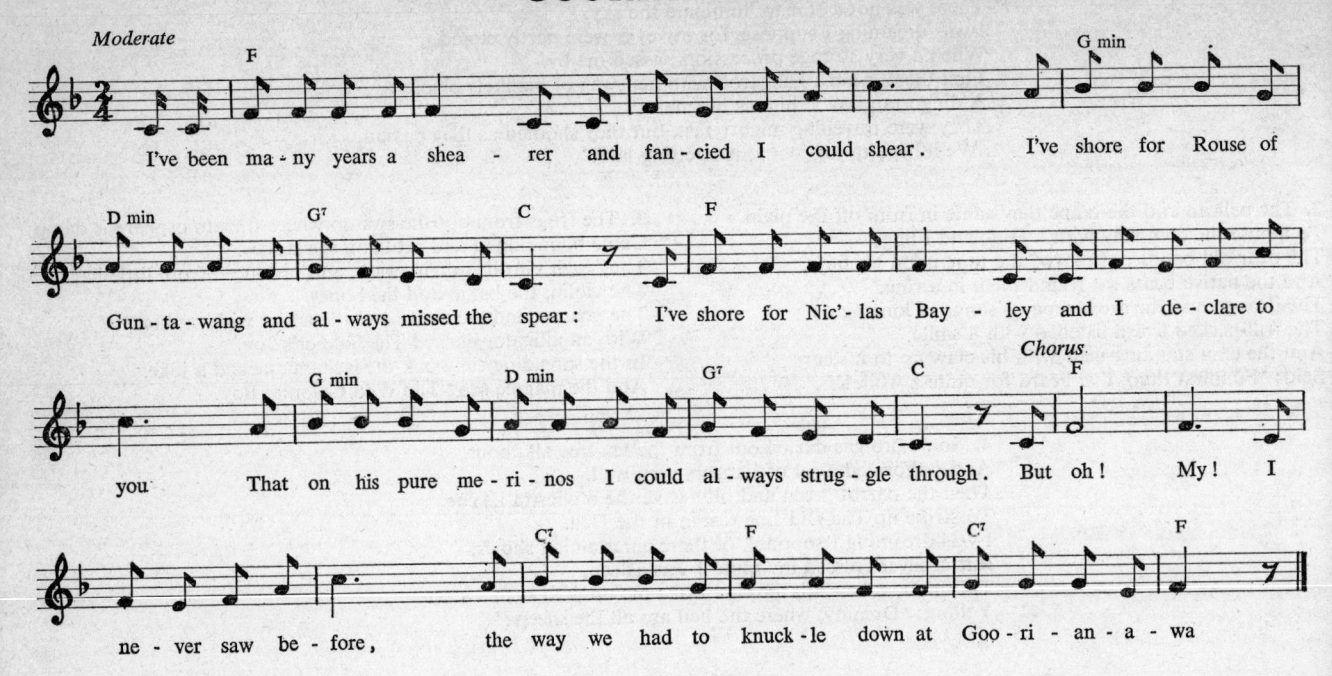

Moderate

I've been many years a shearer and fancied I could shear. I've shore for Rouse of Guntawang and always missed the spear: I've shore for Nic'las Bayley and I declare to you That on his pure merinos I could always struggle through. But oh! My! I never saw before, the way we had to knuckle down at Goo-ri-an-a-wa

126

1. I've been many years a shearer, and fancied I could shear,
I've shore for Rouse of Guntawang and always missed the spear;
I've shore for Nicholas Bayley, and I declare to you
That on his pure merinos I could always struggle through.

Chorus: But, oh! My! I never saw before,
      The way we had to knuckle down at Goorianawa.

2. I've been shearing down the Bogan, as far as Dandaloo;
For good old Reid of Tabretong I've often cut a few.
Haddon Rig and Quambone, and even Wingadee,
I could close my shears at six o'clock with a quiet century.

3. I've been shearing on the Goulburn side and down at Douglas Park,
Where every day 'twas 'Wool away!' and Toby did his work.
I've shore for General Stewart, whose tomb is on The Mount,
And the sprees I've had with Scrammy Jack are more than I can count.

4. I've shore for John McMaster down on Rockedgial Creek,
And I could always dish him up with thirty score a week.
I've shore at Terramungamine and on the Talbragar
And I ran McDermott for the cobbler when we shore at Buckingbar.

5. I've been shearing at Eugowra, I'll never forget the name,
Where Gardiner robbed the escort that from the Lachlan came.
I've shore for Bob Fitzgerald down at the Dabee Rocks,
McPhillamy of Charlton and Mister Henry Cox.

6. That was in the good old days – you might have heard them say,
How Skellycorn from Bathurst rode to Sydney in a day.
But now I'm broken-mouthed and my shearing's at an end,
And though they called me Whalebone, I was never known to bend.

Last Chorus: But spare me flamin' days, I never saw before,
      The way we had to knuckle down at Goorianawa.

WIDGEGOARA JOE
(The Backblock Shearer)

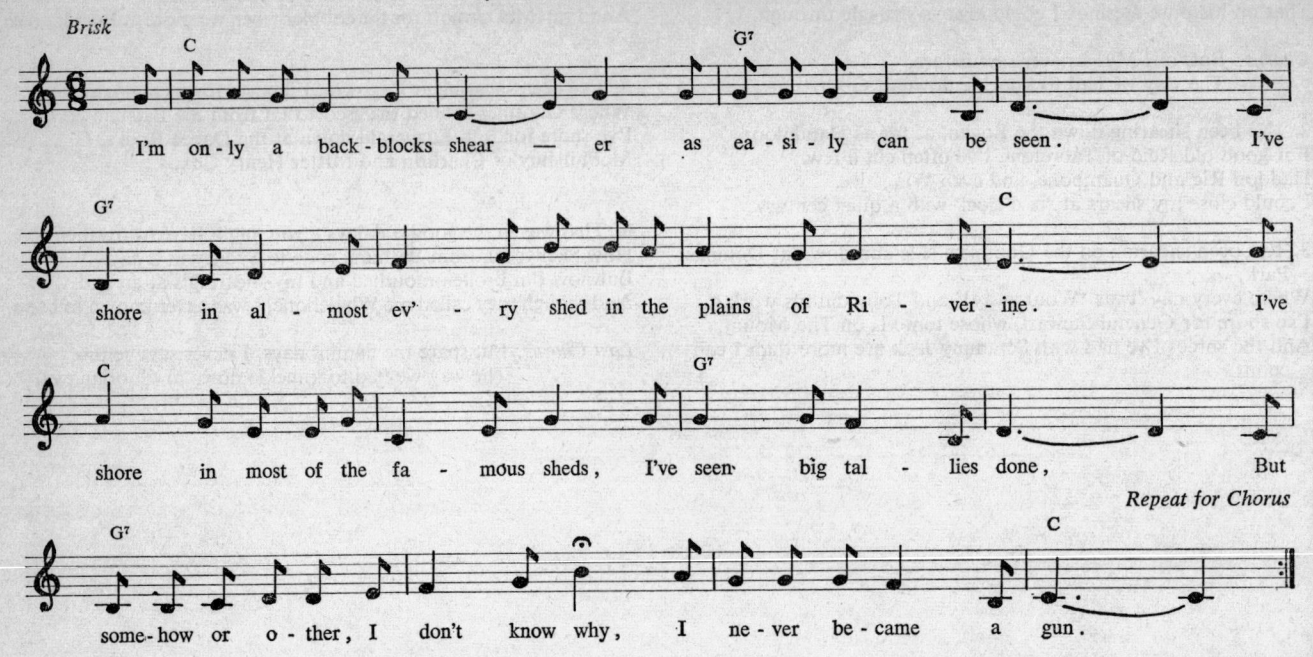

Brisk

I'm only a back-blocks shear — er as easily can be seen. I've shore in almost ev'ry shed in the plains of Riverine. I've shore in most of the famous sheds, I've seen big tallies done, But some-how or other, I don't know why, I never became a gun.

Repeat for Chorus

1. I'm only a backblocks shearer, as easily can be seen,
I've shore in almost every shed in the plains of Riverine.
I've shore in most of the famous sheds, I've seen big tallies done,
But somehow or other, I don't know why, I never became a gun.

Chorus: Hurrah my boys, my shears are set, I feel both fit and well;
Tomorrow will find me at my pen, when the gaffer rings the bell.
With Haydon's patent thumb-guards fixed, and both my blades pulled back;
Tomorrow I go with my siding blow for a century or the sack.

2. I've opened up the windpipe straight, I've opened behind the ear;
I've practised every possible style in which a man can shear;
I've studied all the cuts and drives of the famous men I've met,
But I never succeeded in plastering up those three little figures yet.

3. As the boss walked down this morning, I saw him stare at me,
For I'd mastered Moran's great shoulder-cut, as he could plainly see;
But I've another surprise for him that'll give his nerves a shock –
Tomorrow he'll find that I have mastered Pierce's rang-tang block.

4. If I succeed as I hope to do, then I intend to shear
At the Wagga demonstration which is held there every year!
And there I'll lower the colours, the colours of Mitchell & Co.
Instead of Deeming, you will hear of Widgegoara Joe!

THE BANKS OF THE CONDAMINE

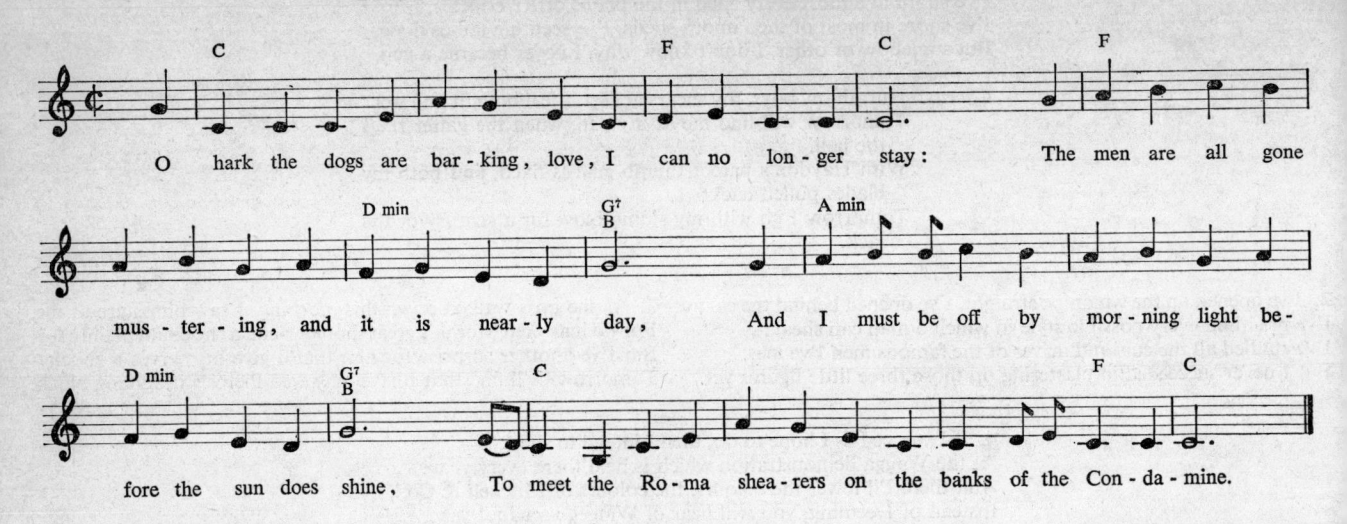

O hark the dogs are barking, love, I can no longer stay: The men are all gone mustering, and it is nearly day, And I must be off by morning light before the sun does shine, To meet the Roma shearers on the banks of the Condamine.

1. MAN: O hark the dogs are barking, love, I can no longer stay;
    The men are all gone mustering, and it is nearly day.
    And I must be off by morning light before the sun does shine,
    To meet the Roma shearers on the banks of the Condamine.

2. GIRL: O Willy, dearest Willy, O let me go with you!
    I'll cut off all my auburn fringe, and be a shearer too;
    I'll cook and count your tally, love, while ringer-O you shine,
    And I'll wash your greasy moleskins on the banks of the Condamine.

3. MAN: O Nancy, dearest Nancy, with me you cannot go!
    The squatters have given orders, love, no woman should do so.
    And your delicate constitution is not equal unto mine,
    To withstand the constant tigering on the banks of the Condamine.

4. GIRL: O Willy, dearest Willy, then stay at home with me;
    We'll take up a selection, and a farmer's wife I'll be.
    I'll help you husk the corn, love, and cook your meals so fine
    You'll forget the ram-stag mutton on the banks of the Condamine.

5. MAN: O Nancy, dearest Nancy, pray do not hold me back!
    Down there the boys are waiting, and I must be on the track.
    So here's a goodbye kiss, love; back home I will incline
    When we've shore the last of the jumbucks on the banks of the Condamine.

THE BANKS OF THE CONDAMINE
(another version)

Hark, hark the dogs are bar-king, my love I must a-way, The lads are all horse-breaking, no long-er can I stay, For I am bound for camp, love, 'tis many a wea-ry mile, To join the jol-ly horse break-ers, out on the Con-da-mine.

1. MAN: Hark, hark the dogs are barking! My love, I must away.
The lads are all horsebreaking, no longer can I stay.
For I am bound for camp, love, 'tis many a weary mile,
To join the jolly horsebreakers out on the Condamine.

2. Oh Nancy, dearest Nancy, with me you cannot be,
For the boss has given his orders no females there to see.
Your waist is far too slender, your fingers are too small,
For you to ride an outlaw if one to you should fall.

3. GIRL: Oh, I'll cut off my yellow locks and go along with you,
And I'll put on the moleskins and be a rider too,
And I will boil the billy while at riding you do shine,
And I'll wash your dirty moleskins on the banks of the Condamine.

4. MAN: No, no, but away on the sandridge I'll think of you with pride;
My hooks they will go freely along the brumby's side.
Your delicate constitution is not equal unto mine,
And you could not eat the damper on the banks of the Condamine.

5. Then when the riding's over, to our bush we will return;
We'll kiss the wives and sweethearts we left behind to mourn.
We'll embrace them in our arms, love, and I'll take you in mine
And I'll tell you of the riding on the banks of the Condamine.

FLASH JACK FROM GUNDAGAI

I've shore at Burrabogie and I've shore at Togan-main,
I've shore at big Willandra and on the old Coleraine,
But before the shearin' was over I've wished myself back again
Shearin' for old Tom Patterson on the One Tree Plain.

All among the wool, boys, all among the wool,
Keep your blades full, boys, keep your blades full.
I can do a respectable tally myself Whenever I like to try,
And they know me round the back blocks as Flash Jack from Gundagai.

Repeat for Chorus

134

1. I've shore at Burrabogie, and I've shore at Toganmain,
I've shore at big Willandra and on the old Coleraine,
But before the shearin' was over I've wished myself back again
Shearin' for old Tom Patterson, on the One Tree Plain.

Chorus: All among the wool, boys, all among the wool,
Keep your blades full boys, keep you blades full.
I can do a respectable tally myself whenever I like to try
And they know me round the backblocks as Flash Jack
from Gundagai.

2. I've shore at big Willandra and I've shore at Tilberoo,
And once I drew my blades, my boys, upon the famed Barcoo,
At Cowan Downs and Trida, as far as Moulamein,
But I always was glad to get back again to the One Tree Plain.

3. I've pinked 'em with the Wolseleys and I've rushed with B-bows, too,
And shaved 'em in the grease, my boys, with the grass seed showing through.
But I never slummed my pen, my lads, whate'er it might contain,
While shearin' for old Tom Patterson, on the One Tree Plain.

4. I've been whalin' up the Lachlan, and I've dossed on Cooper's Creek,
And once I rung Cudjingie shed, and blued it in a week.
But when Gabriel blows his trumpet, lads, I'll catch the morning train,
And I'll push for old Tom Patterson's on the One Tree Plain.

BULLOCKY-O

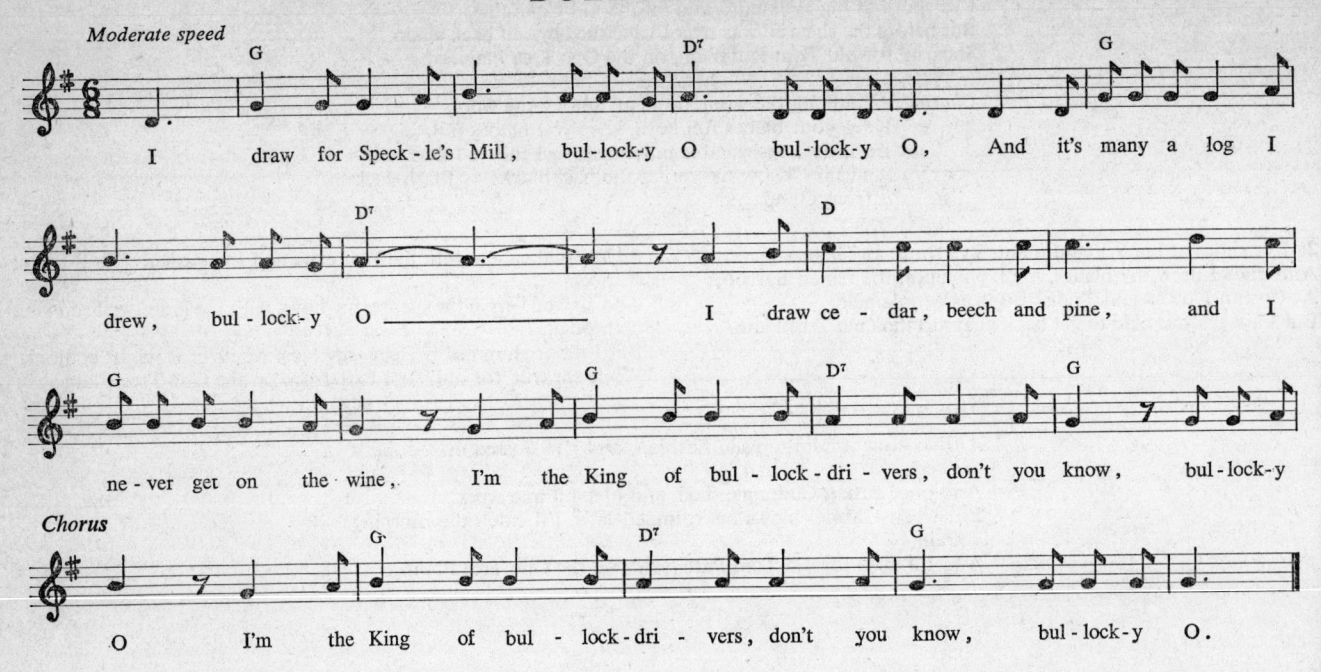

Moderate speed

I draw for Speck-le's Mill, bul-lock-y O bul-lock-y O, And it's many a log I drew, bul-lock-y O ———— I draw ce-dar, beech and pine, and I ne-ver get on the wine, I'm the King of bul-lock-dri-vers, don't you know, bul-lock-y

Chorus

O I'm the King of bul-lock-dri-vers, don't you know, bul-lock-y O.

1. I draw for Speckle's Mill, bullocky-O, bullocky-O,
And it's many a log I drew, bullocky-O.
I draw cedar, beech and pine, and I never get on the wine;
I'm the king of bullock-drivers, don't you know, bullocky-O!

Chorus: I'm the king of bullock-drivers, don't you know,
                                                        bullocky-O!

2. There's Guinea and Anderson too, bullocky-O, bullocky-O,
And it's many a log they drew, bullocky-O.
I can give 'em a thousand feet, axe 'em square and never cheat;
I'm the king of bullock-drivers, don't you know, bullocky-O!

3. There's Wapples too, he brags, bullocky-O, bullocky-O,
Of his forty rawboned stags, bullocky-O.
I can tell you it's no slander when I say I raise their dander,
When they hear the crack of me whip, bullocky-O, bullocky-O.

THE SHEEPWASHER

1. When first I took the Western track, 'twas many years ago,
No master then stood up so high, no servant stood so low;
But now the squatters, puffed with pride, do treat us with disdain.
Lament with me the bygone days that will not come again.

2. I had a pair of ponies once, to bear me on my road;
I earned a decent cheque at times, and blued it like a lord.
But lonely now I hump my drum in sunshine and in rain,
Lamenting on the bygone days that will not come again.

3. Let bushmen all in unity combine with heart and hand
Till bloody cringing poverty is driven from our land;
Let never Queensland come to know the tyrant's ball and chain,
And workers all in time to come their vanished rights regain.

BILL THE BULLOCKY

Tune: Camooweal Races

1. As I came down through Conroy's Gap,
     I heard a maiden cry,
   'There goes old Bill the Bullocky,
     He's bound for Gundagai!
   A better bullock-driver never
     Cracked an honest crust;
   A kinder-hearted driver never
     Dragged a whip through dust.'

2. His team got bogged at Five-Mile Creek;
     Bill lashed and cried and swore,
   'If Nobby don't haul us out of this
     I'll speak to him no more!'
   So Nobby strained, and broke the yoke,
     And poked out Baldy's eye,
   And the dog sat on the tucker-box
     Five miles from Gundagai.

THE OLD BULLOCK DRAY

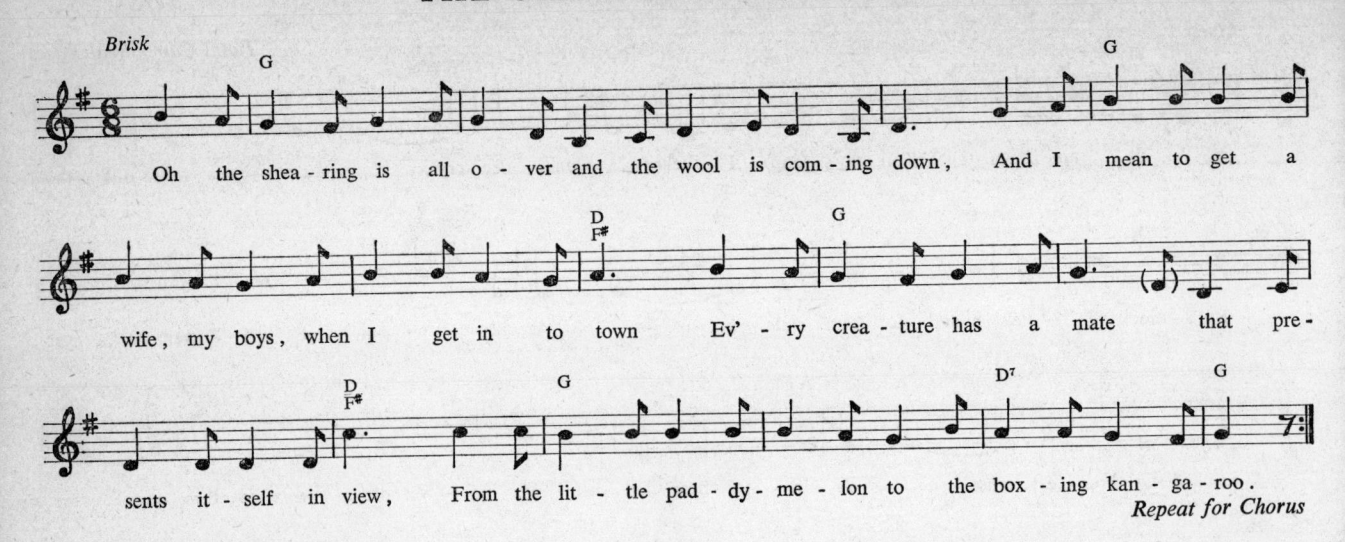

Brisk

Oh the shea-ring is all o-ver and the wool is com-ing down, And I mean to get a wife, my boys, when I get in to town Ev'-ry crea-ture has a mate that pre-sents it-self in view, From the lit-tle pad-dy-me-lon to the box-ing kan-ga-roo.

Repeat for Chorus

1. Oh the shearing is all over and the wool is coming down,
And I mean to get a wife, my boys, when I get in to town.
Every creature has a mate that presents itself in view,
From the little paddymelon to the boxing kangaroo.

Chorus: So it's roll up your blankets and let's make a push!
    I'll take you up the counteree and show you the bush.
    I'll be bound you won't get such a chance another day,
    So come and take possession of the old bullock dray.

2. I've been saving up my cheques and I mean to buy a team,
So when I get a wife, my boys, we'll be all serene.
I'll be calling at the Factory – they say there's no delay –
And getting an offsider for the old bullock dray.

3. I can offer beef and damper, and be certain there's enough;
We'll have leatherjackets, johnny-cakes and bucketsfull of duff.
And if anyone fancies fish, I can catch 'em pretty soon,
For we'll bob for barramundies on the banks of the lagoon.

4. We'll be stopping immigration, won't be needing any more,
We'll be raising young colonials by the dozen and the score,
And I wonder what the devil Jack Robertson would say
If he saw us promenading round the old bullock dray.

5. We'll have plenty girls and boys if we give our minds to that;
There'll be flash little Maggie and a buck-jumping Pat,
There'll be Stringybark Josephine and Greenhide Mike,
Oh, my colonial oath, there'll be as many as you like!

6. If the lady doesn't answer, I can bear it with a grin;
I'll go back up the counteree and marry a native gin.
And our friends will come and dance in honour of the day
To the music of the bells around the old bullock dray.

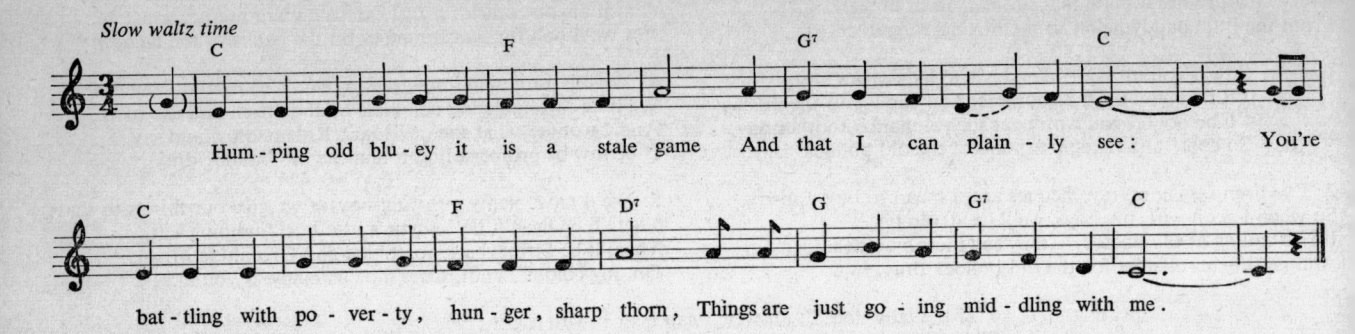

HUMPING OLD BLUEY

Slow waltz time

Hum-ping old blu-ey it is a stale game And that I can plain-ly see: You're bat-tling with po-ver-ty, hun-ger, sharp thorn, Things are just go-ing mid-dling with me.

1. Humping old bluey, it's a stale game,
And that I can plainly see;
You're battling with poverty, hunger, sharp thorn,
Things are just going middling with me.

2. Now the shearing's all over, and I'm such a swell,
I'm riding a very fine hack;
If my friends were to see me, I'm not humping bluey,
I'm pushing a bit further back.

3. Humping your drum, that after rum,
Wasting your young life away;
You're battling with poverty, hunger, sharp thorn,
Things are just going middling, I say.

I'VE JUST COME FROM SYDNEY

1. Oh I've just come from Sydney across the range of mountains
   Where the nannygoats and the billygoats and the moocows do dwell;
   Oh I've just come in search of a pretty little maiden,
   Though where she is now I ca-a-an not tell.

2. Oh how shall I find her? To you I'll describe her:
   She wears a flannel petticoat and a hat upon her head;
   She sleeps when she's walking and snores when she's talking,
   And her clothes are all marked with a W X Y Z.

3. Oh where shall I find her? She ran away with a Chinaman!
   Farewell to the nannygoats and the billygoats so high,
   Farewell to the moocows! By the seaside I'll wander,
   And in its cold waters I'll lay me down and . . . (*spoken*) get up again.

143

THE REEDY LAGOON

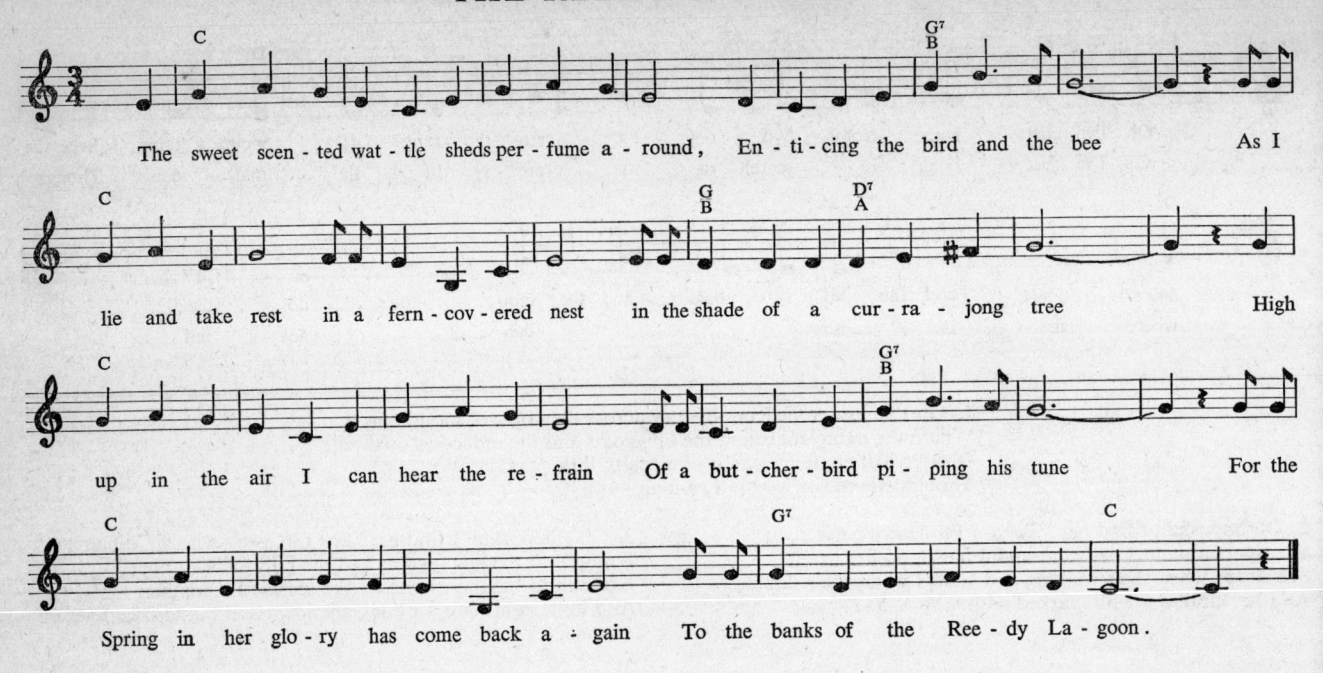

The sweet scented wattle sheds perfume around, Enticing the bird and the bee As I lie and take rest in a fern-covered nest in the shade of a currajong tree High up in the air I can hear the refrain Of a butcher-bird piping his tune For the Spring in her glory has come back again To the banks of the Reedy Lagoon.

1. The sweet-scented wattle sheds perfume around,
   Enticing the bird and the bee,
As I lie and take rest in a fern-covered nest
   In the shade of a currajong tree.
High up in the air I can hear the refrain
   Of a butcherbird piping his tune,
For the Spring in her glory has come back again
   To the banks of the Reedy Lagoon.

2. I've carried my bluey for many a mile,
   My boots are worn out at the toes,
And I'm dressing this season in different style
   From what I did last year, God knows!
My cooking utensils, I'm sorry to say,
   Consist of a knife and a spoon;
And I've dry bread and tea in a battered Jack-Shea
   On the banks of the Reedy Lagoon.

3. Oh where is poor Frankie (and how he could ride!)
   And Johnny the kindhearted boy?
They tell me that lately he's taken a bride
   A Benedick's life to enjoy.
And Mac the big Scotsman? I once heard him say
   He wrestled the famous Muldoon.
But they're all far away, and I'm lonely today
   On the banks of the Reedy Lagoon.

4. Oh where is the lady I often caressed,
   The girl with the sad dreamy eyes?
She pillows her head on another man's breast
   Who tells her the very same lies!
My bed she would hardly be willing to share
   Where I camp in the light of the moon!
But it's little I care, for I couldn't keep square,
   On the banks of the Reedy Lagoon.

WILD ROVER NO MORE

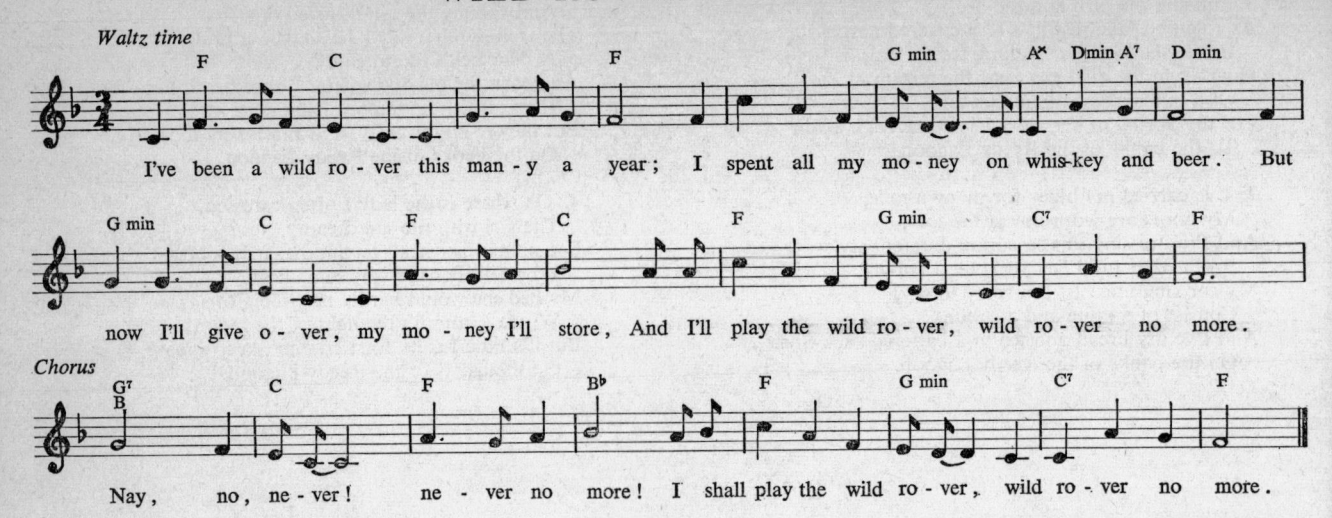

Waltz time

I've been a wild rover this many a year; I spent all my money on whiskey and beer. But now I'll give over, my money I'll store, And I'll play the wild rover, wild rover no more.

Chorus

Nay, no, never! never no more! I shall play the wild rover, wild rover no more.

1. I've been a wild rover this many a year;
I spent all my money on whisky and beer.
But now I'll give over, my money I'll store,
And I'll play the wild rover, wild rover no more.

Chorus: Nay, no, never! never no more!
I shall play the wild rover, wild rover no more.

2. I went to a shanty I used to frequent,
And I told the landlady my money was spent.
I asked her for credit, she answered me 'Nay,
Such custom as yours I can get any day.'

3. Then out of my pocket I drew sovereigns bright;
The landlady opened her eyes at the sight!
She said 'I have whisky and wines of the best,
For the things I was saying were only in jest.'

4. I'll go to my parents, tell them what I've done,
And beg them to pardon their prodigal son;
And if they forgive me as they've done before,
I shall play the wild rover, wild rover no more.

NOTES

THE QUEENSLAND DROVER (THE OVERLANDER)

Known from childhood. The first tune is one that I must have learnt from my father, and heard again from Vance Palmer in 1950. Both men would have picked it up in southern central Queensland at about the same time, *circa* 1900. The tune given in Palmer and Sutherland is not exactly the same. The second tune, with verses agreeing so closely as to be printable as one single version, was sung to me by Mrs Webb, late of Cairns, in 1962. It appears to be a descendent of the tune 'Dearest Mae' given by Anderson. Text is from *Bandicoot Ballads*.

THE UNION BOY

Here is another of John Meredith's brilliant finds: recorded at Gulgong in 1956 from a shearer, Bill Coughlin, who learnt it at Cassilis, New South Wales, during the shearing strike in 1902. From the Bush Music Club, Sydney.

THE RYEBUCK SHEARER

From *Singabout*, Vol. 2, No. 1. Bill Lewis has given me fragments of another ballad to the same tune, beginning:

> Of a squatter outback on the Gulf I've heard
> With a face like a dried-up buffalo turd ...

LADIES OF BRISBANE (THE DROVER'S SONG and AUGATHELIA STATION)

Given in two versions to illustrate the process of 'collective re-creation'. Hugh Anderson has tracked down the original parody of 'Spanish Ladies' with the tune in the major mode; it was printed in *The Boomerang* in 1891. The more proletarian version with the tune in the minor was a favourite of the late Dr Dalley-Scarlett; it was collected by the Queensland Folklore Society and printed in the *Queensland Pocket Songbook*.

A slightly different text and a totally different tune (collected in Victoria by Ron Edwards) appeared as a *Bandicoot Ballad*. The differences between texts are worth study. I have no clue to the purpose of the quotation marks around 'old cattle station' in the first version given here, or to the identity of Jack Smith the Don.

THE DROVER'S DREAM

From *Bandicoot Ballads* via the *Queensland Pocket Songbook*. There are many variant verses, from as far south as Victoria (reported by Miss Thea McKenzie) and as far north as Darwin (according to Geoff Wills), but these are a fair sample.

GOORIANAWA

From *Singabout*, Vol. 1, No. 3. Hugh Anderson has turned up a shorter version printed in *The Lone Hand* in 1912, and comments that Paterson had appealed in vain for a copy of the same song in 1905. Paterson's reference makes it plain that the *Lone Hand* version is not the original. I recommend that those interested should hear this sung by 'Duke' Tritton on the Wattle record 'Australian Traditional Singers'.

WIDGEGOARA JOE (THE BACKBLOCK SHEARER)

The *Bandicoot Ballads* version corrects what seem to be mistakes in the original printing in *Speewah*. Widgegoara is the name on the sign-post: most maps accept Widgeegoara. The spelling Widgee-goweera is either 'phonetic' (like 'Melbne' for Melbourne) or obsolete. The other question concerns the *Speewah* printing in last chorus line, 'sardine blow'. All the shearers I have been able to consult are certain that this means the 'siding blow', which is the 'long blow'.

A variant has been collected by the Folklore Society of Victoria in which the place-name has been corrupted to 'Widgegowarmy'.

THE BANKS OF THE CONDAMINE

The shearer version is from the *Queensland Pocket Songbook*. The horsebreaker version was given to me by Miss Alison Jordan of Kiata, Victoria, and its tune by Geoff and Nancy Wills who picked it up in the Northern Territory. Palmer and Sutherland print a 32-bar tune, the first sixteen bars of which also appear in *Bandicoot Ballads*, and in a souvenir songbook published by the Australian World Youth Festival Committee, 1951.

FLASH JACK FROM GUNDAGAI

The tune is from the singing of the Queensland Folklore Society, the words from Paterson. The different chorus-length in Paterson's version suggests that another tune may have been used sometimes.

BULLOCKY-O

From the *Queensland Pocket Songbook*, collected by the Queensland Folklore Society from Cyril Duncan, Nerang, Queensland.

THE SHEEPWASHER

From *Bandicoot Ballads*, reprinted with annotations in the *Queensland Pocket Songbook*. Paterson prints a very much longer version with the note that the tune is 'The Bonnie Irish Boy'. Anderson prints Paterson's version with a triple-time tune which he calls 'The Bonnie Irish Boy', and the *Overlander Songbook* follows suit. The trouble is that this triple-time tune clearly belongs to verses of different metrical pattern. I suggest that the tune Paterson may have had in mind is the one printed in Joyce's *Old Irish Folk-music and Songs* as 'The Irish Girl', also known as 'The Bonny Labouring Boy'. In nearly all known texts of this song, the first verse ends with the tag line: 'my bonny Irish boy'; so confusion is quite possible.

A variant of the Anderson/*Overlander* tune is the one I have used in this book for 'My Name is Ben Hall'.

BILL THE BULLOCKY

From *Bandicoot Ballads*. Composite. The tune, 'Camooweal Races', was collected by Geoff Wills, without words. The words were collected, in somewhat more exuberant language but without a tune, by John Meredith.

THE OLD BULLOCK DRAY

This is the version I have been singing myself, and I suppose I have incorporated verses or lines from other singers. Two other versions are printed by Stewart and Keesing.

The tune is generally set down as American – 'Turkey in the Straw' – but I have heard something very much like it used in England for 'The Durham Reel'. A different tune and some magnificent variant words are in Palmer and Sutherland *Old Australian Bush Ballads*.

HUMPING OLD BLUEY

From *Singabout*, Vol. 3, No. 3. A longer version, without tune, is in one of the Bill Bowyang reciters.

I'VE JUST COME FROM SYDNEY

From the *Queensland Pocket Songbook*, collected in Darling Downs by Hilda Lane.

THE REEDY LAGOON

From the *Queensland Pocket Songbook* where full details of source are given.

WILD ROVER NO MORE

From the singing of Bob Myles, at Currumbin, South Queensland. The tune is also still current in northern England. Paterson's version is only slightly different.

6
THE POETS

THERE have always been a few poets who stand with one foot in the camp of folksong and the other in that of literature. I have not tried to include all of them here; some of them are represented in other sections of the book.

Frank Macnamara's surviving MS poems are not sung; the songs in which he may possibly have had a hand are consequently classed with the anonymous convict songs. John McGuire wrote but the one ballad in his life and never classed himself as a literary man; so I have left him in Section 3.

Robert Lowe and Charles Flower are both here, but Charles Thatcher is not. All three men have achieved a certain status in the bush singers' repertory, but Thatcher's work is readily available in Hugh Anderson's two books, *Colonial Ballads* and *The Colonial Minstrel*.

Banjo Paterson and Henry Lawson are here by right. Both men wrote poems which are practically indistinguishable from the bush songs on which they were nourished in their youth. Furthermore, folktunes sprang up to carry these poems, and that seems to me to legitimatize their inclusion here.

My own ballad is in this section because it has been the means of preserving a rather fine tune that really belongs to a lost Kelly ballad. The pieces by Wakefield and Lilley are just a reminder that Ted Harrington (bless him!) is far from deserving the title 'last of the balladists'!

The notes to each song in this part are on page 175 of this book.

THE COMMISSIONER

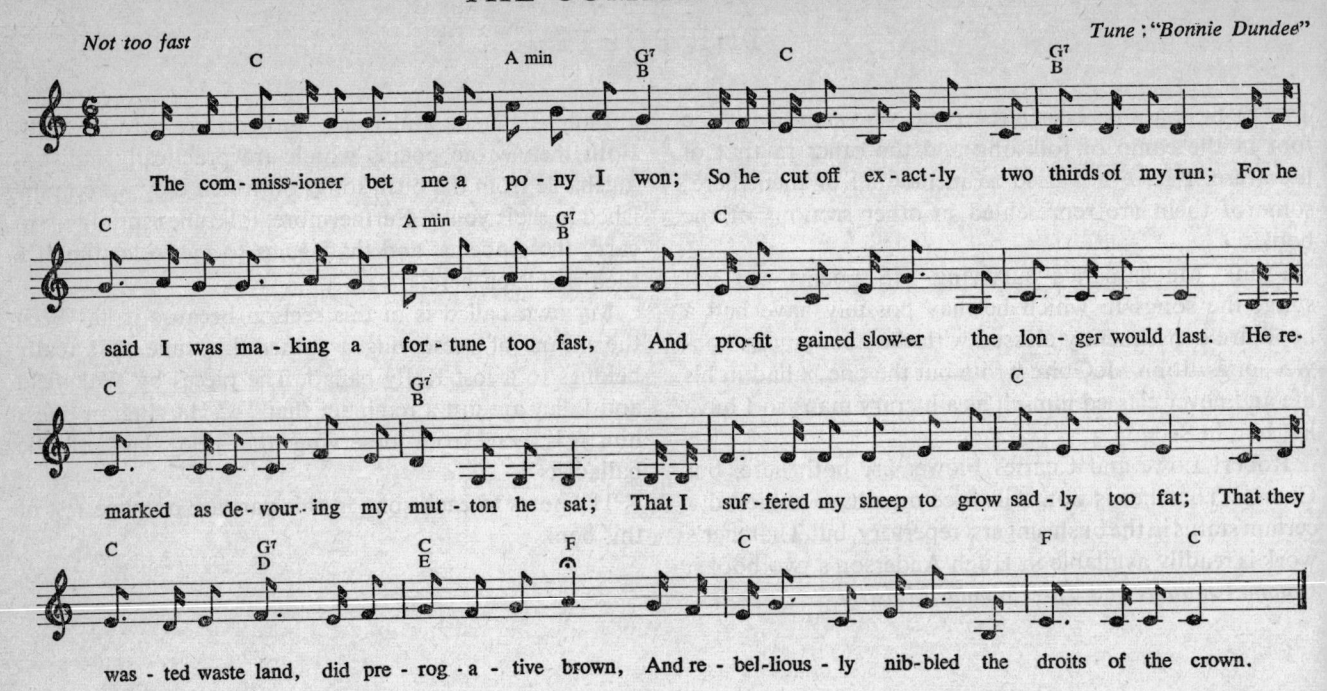

Tune: "Bonnie Dundee"

Not too fast

The com-miss-ioner bet me a po-ny I won; So he cut off ex-act-ly two thirds of my run; For he said I was ma-king a for-tune too fast, And pro-fit gained slow-er the lon-ger would last. He re-marked as de-vour-ing my mut-ton he sat; That I suf-fered my sheep to grow sad-ly too fat; That they was-ted waste land, did pre-rog-a-tive brown, And re-bel-lious-ly nib-bled the droits of the crown.

1. The commissioner bet me a pony – I won;
So he cut off exactly two thirds of my run;
For he said I was making a fortune too fast,
And profit gained slower the longer would last.
He remarked, as devouring my mutton he sat,
That I suffered my sheep to grow sadly too fat;
That they wasted waste land, did prerogative brown,
And rebelliously nibbled the droits of the Crown.

2. The commissioner fined me because I forgot
To return an old ewe that was ill of the rot,
And a poor wry-necked lamb that we kept as a pet.
He said it was treason such things to forget!
The commissioner pounded my cattle because
They had mumbled the scrub with their famishing jaws
On the part of the run he had taken away;
And he sold them by auction their costs to defray.

3. The Border Police they were out all the day
To look for some thieves who had ransacked my dray;
But the thieves they continued in quiet and peace,
For they'd robbed it themselves, had the Border Police!
When the white thieves had left me, the black thieves appeared,
My shepherds they waddied, my cattle they speared;
But for fear of my licence, I said not a word,
For I knew it was gone if the Government heard.

4. The commissioner's bosom with anger was filled
Against me because my poor shepherd was killed;
So he straight took away the last third of my run
And got it transferred to the name of his son.
The son had from Cambridge been lately expelled,
And his licence for preaching most justly withheld!
But this is no cause, the commissioner says,
Why he should not be granted a licence to graze.

5. The Governor told me I justly was served,
That commissioners never from duty had swerved;
But that if I'd a fancy for any more land
For one pound an acre he'd plenty on hand.
I'm not very proud! I can dig in a bog,
Feed pigs, or for firewood can cut up a log,
Clean shoes, riddle cinders, or help to boil down –
Or whatever you please but graze lands of the Crown!

THE BROKEN-DOWN SQUATTER

Waltz time.

Come, Stumpy, old man, we must shift while we can: All your mates in the paddock are dead. Let us bid our farewells to Glen Eva's sweet dells, And the place where your lordship was bred.

Together we'll roam from our drought-stricken home— It seems hard that such things have to be, But it's hard on a horse when he's nought for a boss, But a broken down squatter like me.

154

Chorus

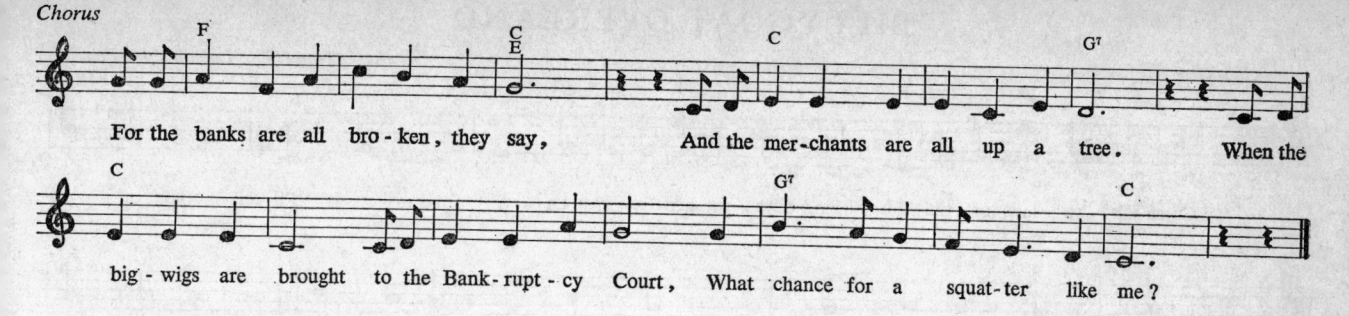

For the banks are all broken, they say, And the merchants are all up a tree. When the bigwigs are brought to the Bankruptcy Court, What chance for a squatter like me?

2. No more shall we muster the river for fats,
Or spiel on the Fifteen Mile Plain,
Or rip through the scrub by the light of the moon,
Or see the old stockyard again.
Leave the slip-panels down, it won't matter much now,
There are none but the crows left to see,
Perching gaunt on yon pine, as though longing to dine
On a broken-down squatter like me.

3. When the country was cursed with the drought at its worst
And the cattle were dying in scores,
Though down on my luck, I kept up my pluck
Thinking justice might temper the laws.
But the farce has been played and the Government aid
Ain't extended to squatters, old son,
When my money was spent, they doubled the rent,
And resumed the best half of the run.

4. 'Twas done without reason, for leaving the season,
No squatter could stand such a rub,
For it's useless to squat when the rents are so hot
That you can't save the price of your grub;
And there's not much to choose 'twixt the banks and the screws
Once a fellow gets up a tree.
No odds what I feel, there's no court of appeal
For a broken-down squatter like me.

Chorus: For the banks are all broken, they say,
And the merchants are all up a tree.
When the bigwigs are brought
To the Bankruptcy Court,
What chance for a squatter like me?

155

BILLYGOAT OVERLAND

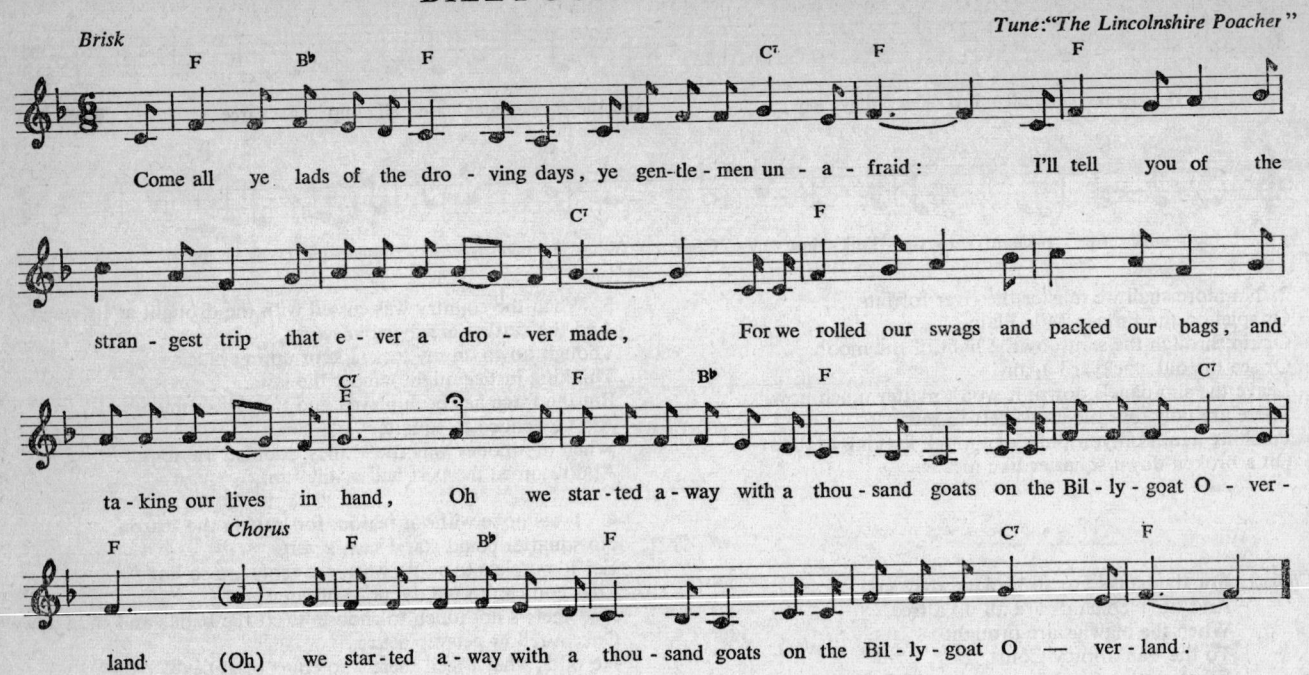

Tune: "The Lincolnshire Poacher"

Brisk

Come all ye lads of the dro-ving days, ye gen-tle-men un-a-fraid: I'll tell you of the stran-gest trip that e-ver a dro-ver made, For we rolled our swags and packed our bags, and ta-king our lives in hand, Oh we star-ted a-way with a thou-sand goats on the Bil-ly-goat O-ver-land

Chorus

(Oh) we star-ted a-way with a thou-sand goats on the Bil-ly-goat O — ver-land.

1. Come all ye lads of the droving days, ye gentlemen unafraid;
I'll tell you of the strangest trip that ever a drover made.
For we rolled our swags and packed our bags, and taking our lives in hand,
Oh, we started away with a thousand goats on the Billygoat Overland.

2. There wasn't a fence that'ld hold the mob, to keep 'em from their desires;
They skipped along the top of the posts and cakewalked on the wires;
And whenever the lanes were bare of grass and the paddocks were nice and green,
Oh, the goats they travelled outside the lanes, and we rode in between!

3. The squatters started to drive them back, but that was no good at all!
The horses ran for the lick of their lives from scent that was like a wall!
And never a dog had pluck enough in front of the mob to stand,
And face the charge of a thousand goats on the Billygoat Overland.

4. We found we were hundreds over strength when we started to count the mob;
And they put us in jail for a crowd of thieves that travelled to steal and rob.
For every goat between here and Bourke that scented our spicy band
Had left his home and his friends to join the Billygoat Overland.

TRAVELLING DOWN THE CASTLEREAGH

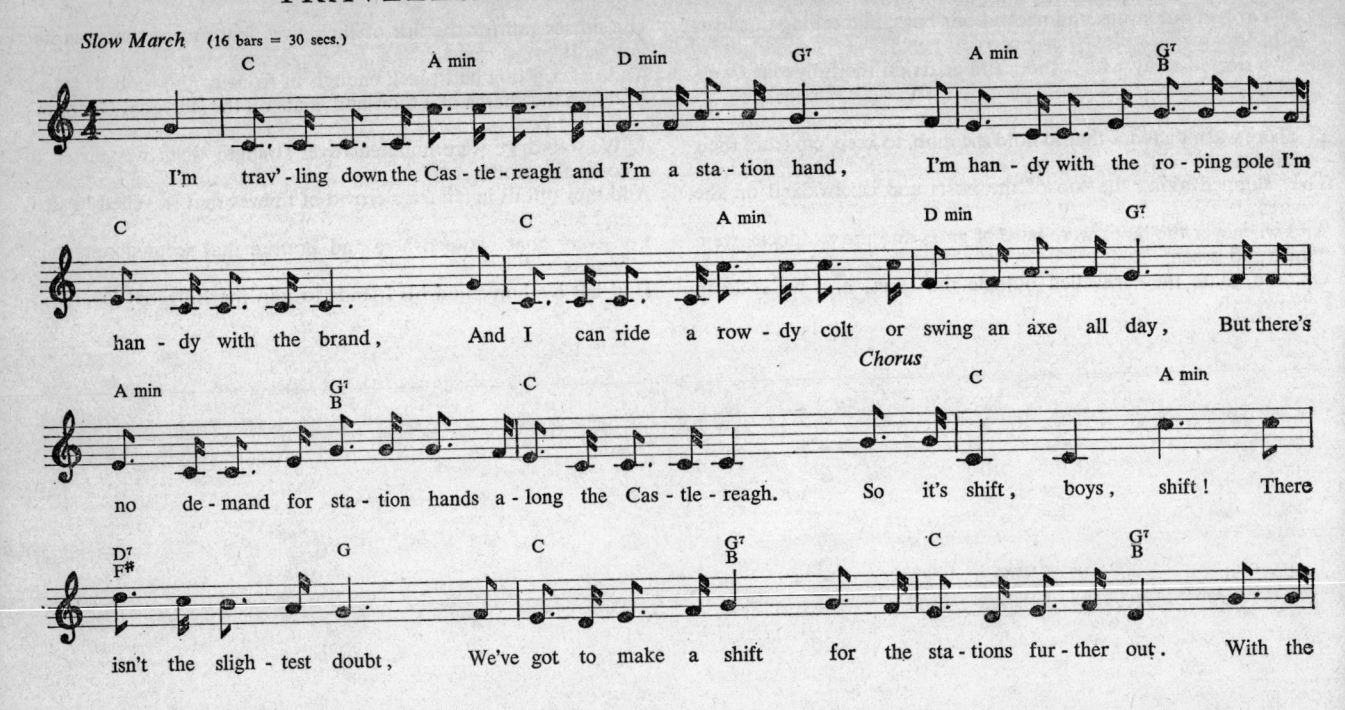

Slow March (16 bars = 30 secs.)

I'm trav'-ling down the Cas-tle-reagh and I'm a sta-tion hand, I'm han-dy with the ro-ping pole I'm han-dy with the brand, And I can ride a row-dy colt or swing an axe all day, But there's no de-mand for sta-tion hands a-long the Cas-tle-reagh.

Chorus

So it's shift, boys, shift! There isn't the sligh-test doubt, We've got to make a shift for the sta-tions fur-ther out. With the pack horse run-ning af-ter, for he fol-lows like a dog, We must strike a-cross the coun-try at the old jig-jog.

1. I'm travelling down the Castlereagh, and I'm a station-hand,
I'm handy with the roping pole, I'm handy with the brand,
And I can ride a rowdy colt, or swing an axe all day,
But there's no demand for station-hands along the Castlereagh.

Chorus: So it's shift, boys, shift! There isn't the slightest doubt
We've got to make a shift for the stations further out.
With the packhorse running after, for he follows like a dog,
We must strike across the country at the old jig-jog.

2. I asked a cove for shearing once along the Marthaguy:
'We shear non-union here,' says he. 'I call it scab,' says I.
I looked along the shearing floor before I turned to go –
There were eight or ten non-union men a-shearing in a row!

Chorus: It was shift, boys, shift! There wasn't the slightest doubt
It was time to make a shift with the leprosy about.
So I saddled up my horses and I whistled to my dog,
And we left his scabby station at the old jig-jog.

3. I went to Illawarra where my brother's got a farm;
He has to ask the landlord's leave before he lifts his arm:
The landlord owns the countryside, man, woman, dog and cat,
They haven't the cheek to dare to speak without they touch their hat.

Chorus: It was shift, boys, shift! There wasn't the slightest doubt
The little landlord-god and I would soon have fallen out.
Was I to touch my hat to him, was I his blooming dog?
So I makes for up the country at the old jig-jog.

4. It's time that I was moving, I've a mighty way to go
Till I drink artesian water from a thousand feet below;
Till I meet the overlanders with the cattle coming down –
I'll work a while and make a pile, then have a spree in town.

Chorus: So it's shift, boys, shift! There isn't the slightest doubt
We've got to make a shift for the stations further out.
With the packhorse running after, for he follows like a dog,
We can cross a lot of country at the old jig-jog.

WALTZING MATILDA
(The Cowan version)

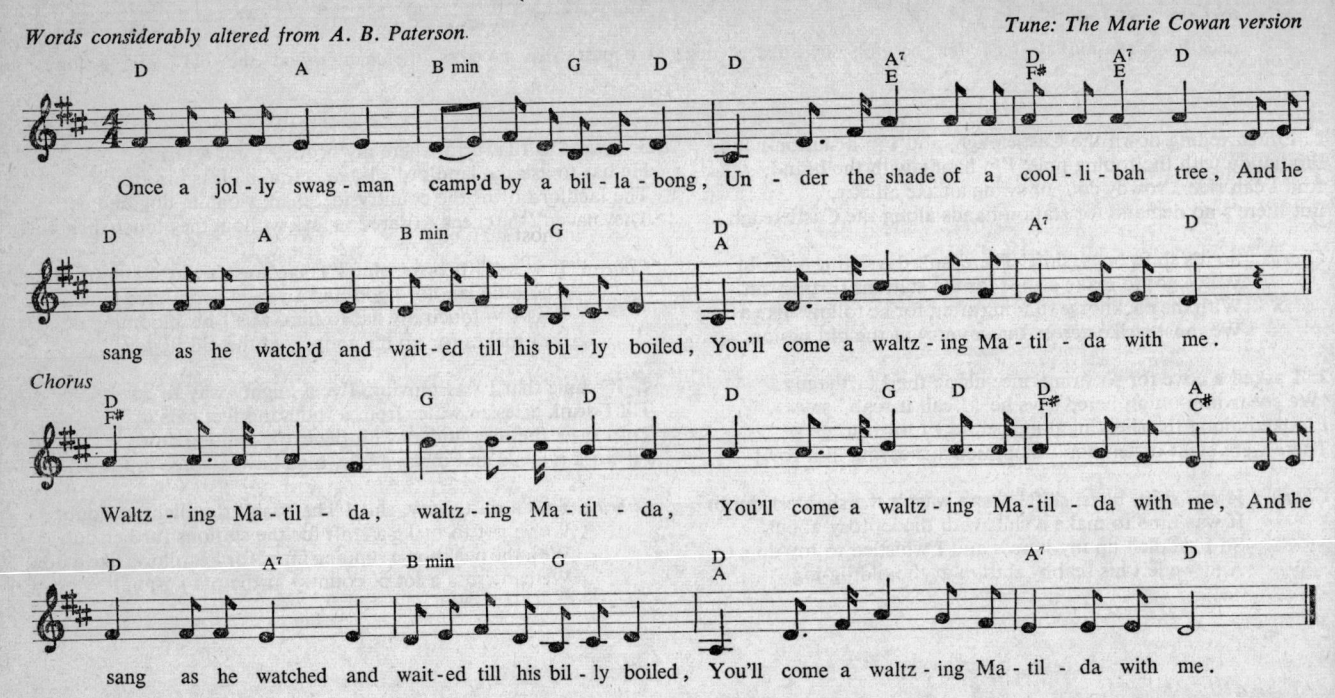

Words considerably altered from A. B. Paterson. *Tune: The Marie Cowan version*

Once a jol-ly swag-man camp'd by a bil-la-bong, Un-der the shade of a cool-li-bah tree, And he sang as he watch'd and wait-ed till his bil-ly boiled, You'll come a waltz-ing Ma-til-da with me.

Chorus

Waltz-ing Ma-til-da, waltz-ing Ma-til-da, You'll come a waltz-ing Ma-til-da with me, And he sang as he watched and wait-ed till his bil-ly boiled, You'll come a waltz-ing Ma-til-da with me.

1. Once a jolly swagman camp'd by a billabong,
   Under the shade of a coolibah tree,
And he sang as he watch'd and waited till his billy boiled
   You'll come a waltzing Matilda with me.

Chorus: Waltzing Matilda, Waltzing Matilda,
   You'll come a waltzing Matilda with me,
   And he sang as he watched and waited till his billy boiled
   You'll come a waltzing Matilda with me.

2. Down came a jumbuck to drink at that billabong,
   Up jumped the swagman and grabbed him with glee,
And he sang as he shoved that jumbuck in his tucker bag
   You'll come a waltzing Matilda with me.

Chorus: Waltzing Matilda, Waltzing Matilda,
   You'll come a waltzing Matilda with me,
   And he sang as he shoved that jumbuck in his tucker bag,
   You'll come a waltzing Matilda with me.

3. Up rode the squatter mounted on his thoroughbred
   Down came the troopers, one, two, three,
Whose that jolly jumbuck you've got in your tucker bag
   You'll come a waltzing Matilda with me.

Chorus: Waltzing Matilda, Waltzing Matilda,
   You'll come a waltzing Matilda with me,
   Whose that jolly jumbuck you've got in your tucker bag
   You'll come a waltzing Matilda with me.

4. Up jumped the swagman, sprang into the billabong,
   You'll never catch me alive said he,
And his ghost may be heard as you pass by that billabong
   You'll come a waltzing Matilda with me.

Chorus: Waltzing Matilda, Waltzing Matilda,
   You'll come a waltzing Matilda with me,
   And his ghost may be heard as you pass by that billabong,
   You'll come a waltzing Matilda with me.

WALTZING MATILDA

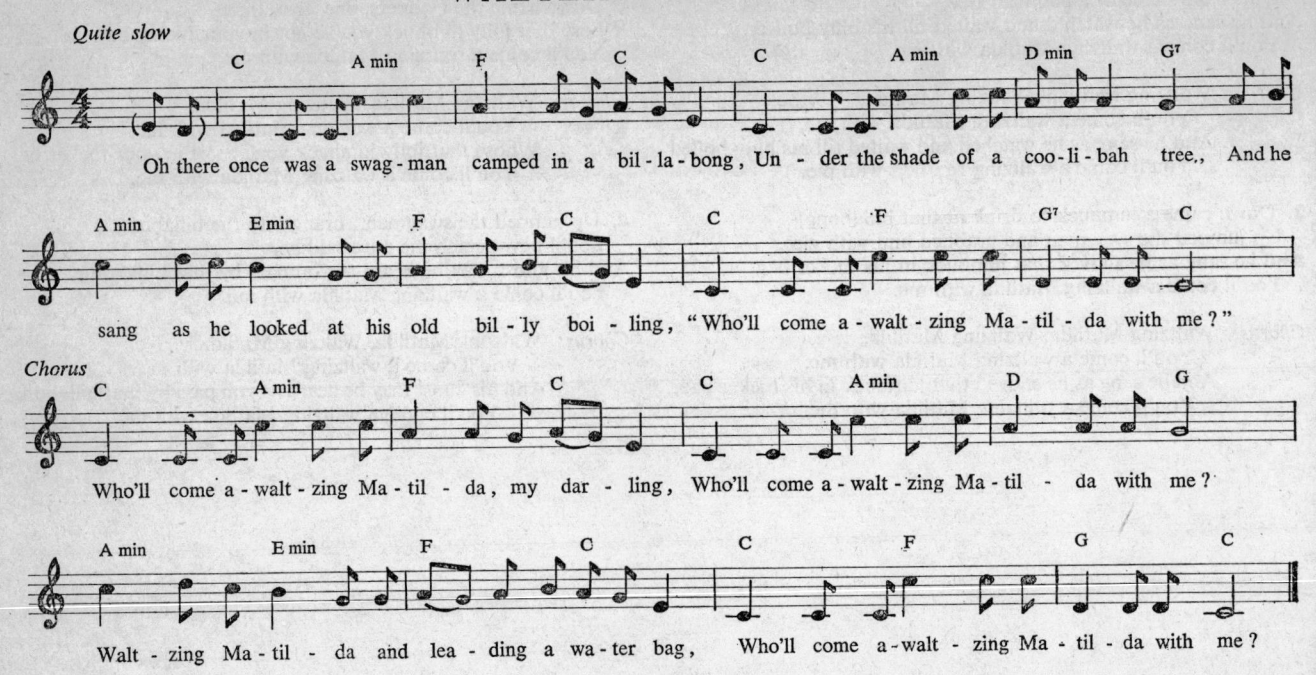

Quite slow

Oh there once was a swag-man camped in a bil-la-bong, Un-der the shade of a coo-li-bah tree., And he sang as he looked at his old bil-ly boi-ling, "Who'll come a-walt-zing Ma-til-da with me?"

Chorus

Who'll come a-walt-zing Ma-til-da, my dar-ling, Who'll come a-walt-zing Ma-til-da with me? Walt-zing Ma-til-da and lea-ding a wa-ter bag, Who'll come a-walt-zing Ma-til-da with me?

1. Oh, there once was a swagman camped in a billabong,
    Under the shade of a coolibah tree;
And he sang as he looked at his old billy boiling,
    'Who'll come a-waltzing Matilda with me?'

Chorus: Who'll come a-waltzing Matilda, my darling?
    Who'll come a-waltzing Matilda with me?
    Waltzing Matilda and leading a water-bag –
    Who'll come a-waltzing Matilda with me?

2. Down came a jumbuck to drink at the water-hole,
    Up jumped the swagman and grabbed him with glee;
And he sang as he stowed him away in his tucker-bag,
    'You'll come a-waltzing Matilda with me.'

3. Down came the Squatter a-riding his thoroughbred;
    Down came Policemen – one, two and three.
'Whose is the jumbuck you've got in the tucker-bag?
    You'll come a-waltzing Matilda with me.'

4. But the swagman he up and he jumped in the water-hole,
    Drowning himself by the coolibah tree;
And his ghost may be heard as it sings in the billabong
    'Who'll come a-waltzing Matilda with me?'

THE SHEARER'S DREAM

Rather slow

Oh, I dreamt I shore in a shear-in' shed An' it was a dream of joy, For ev'ry one of the rous-a-bouts was a girl dressed up as a boy. Dressed up like a page in a pan-to-mime, the pret-ti-est ev-er seen, They had flax-en hair, they had coal-black hair and e-ve-ry shade be-tween.

1. Oh, I dreamt I shore in a shearin'-shed, and it was a dream of joy,
For every one of the rouseabouts was a girl dressed up as a boy –
Dressed up like a page in a pantomime, the prettiest ever seen –
They had flaxen hair, they had coal-black hair – and every shade between.

2. The shed was cooled by electric fans that was over every shoot;
The pens was of polished ma-ho-gany, and everything else to suit;
The huts had springs to the mattresses, and the tucker was simply grand,
And every night by the billabong we danced to a German band.

3. Our pay was the wool on the jumbuck's backs, so we shore till all was blue –
The sheep was washed afore they was shore (and the rams was scented too);
And we all of us wept when the shed cut out, in spite of the long, hot days,
For every hour them girls waltzed in with whisky and beer on trays!

4. There was three of them girls to every chap, and as jealous as they could be –
There was three of them girls to every chap, and six of 'em picked on me;
We was draftin' 'em out for the homeward track and sharin' 'em round like steam,
When I woke with my head in the blazin' sun to find 'twas a shearer's dream.

FREEDOM ON THE WALLABY

Aus-tra-li-a's a big coun-try An' Free-dom's hum-ping blu-ey, An' Free-dom's on the wal-la-by, Oh don't you hear 'er coo-ey? She's just be-gun to boo-mer-ang. She'll knock the ty-rants sil-ly, She's go-ing to light an-o-ther fire And boil an-o-ther bil-ly.

1. Australia's a big country
     An' Freedom's humping bluey,
   An' Freedom's on the wallaby,
     Oh, don't you hear 'er cooey?
   She's just begun to boomerang,
     She'll knock the tyrants silly,
   She's going to light another fire
     And boil another billy.

2. Our fathers toiled for bitter bread
     While loafers thrived beside 'em,
   But food to eat and clothes to wear,
     Their native land denied 'em.
   An' so they left that native land
     In spite of their devotion,
   An' so they came, or if they stole,
     Were sent across the ocean.

3. Then Freedom couldn't stand the glare
     Of royalty's regalia,
   She left the loafers where they were
     An' come out to Australia.
   But now across the mighty main
     The chains have come to bind her,
   She little thought to see again
     The wrong she left behind her.

4. Our fathers grubbed to make a home,
     Hard grubbin' 'twas and clearin',
   They wasn't troubled much with lords
     When they was pioneerin'.
   But now that we have made the land
     A garden full of promise,
   Old Greed must crook 'is dirty hand
     An' come ter take it from us.

5. So we must fly a rebel flag
     As others did before us,
   And we must sing a rebel song
     And join in rebel chorus.
   We'll make the tyrants feel the sting
     O' those that they would throttle;
   They needn't say the fault is ours
     If blood should stain the wattle.

167

THE RABBITER

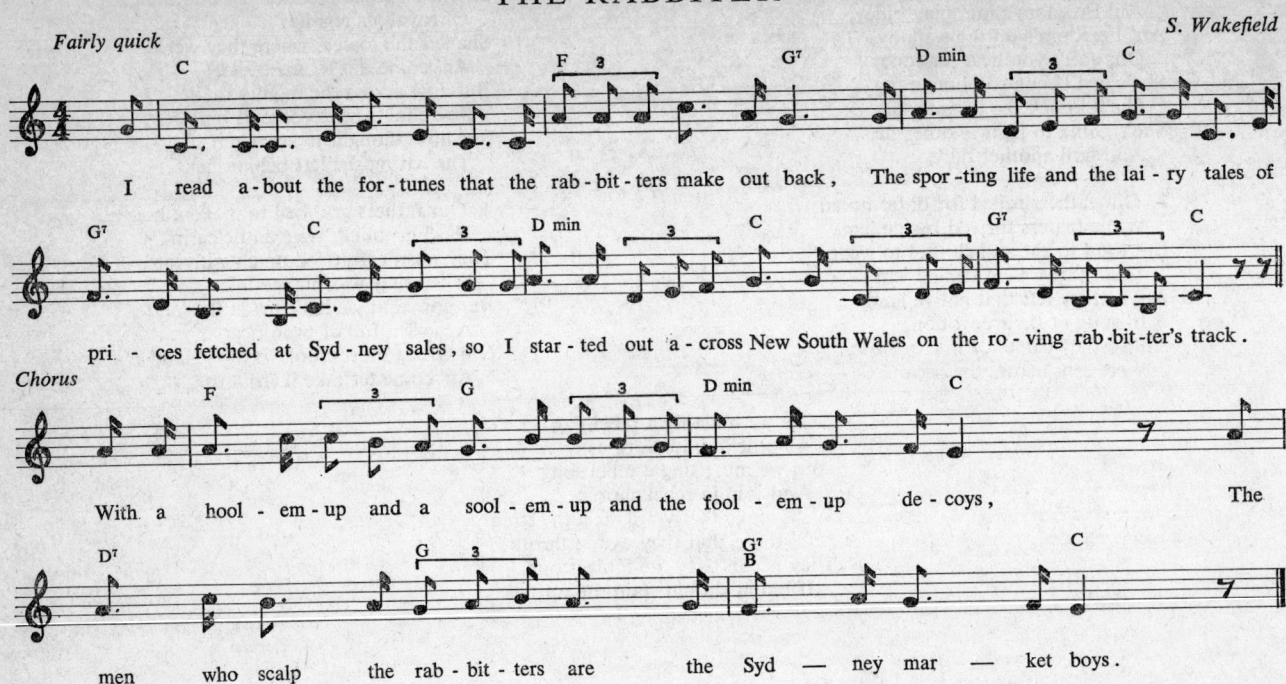

S. Wakefield

Fairly quick

I read about the fortunes that the rabbiters make out back, The sporting life and the lairy tales of prices fetched at Sydney sales, so I started out a-cross New South Wales on the roving rabbiter's track.

Chorus

With a hool-em-up and a sool-em-up and the fool-em-up decoys, The men who scalp the rabbiters are the Syd — ney mar — ket boys.

Final Chorus

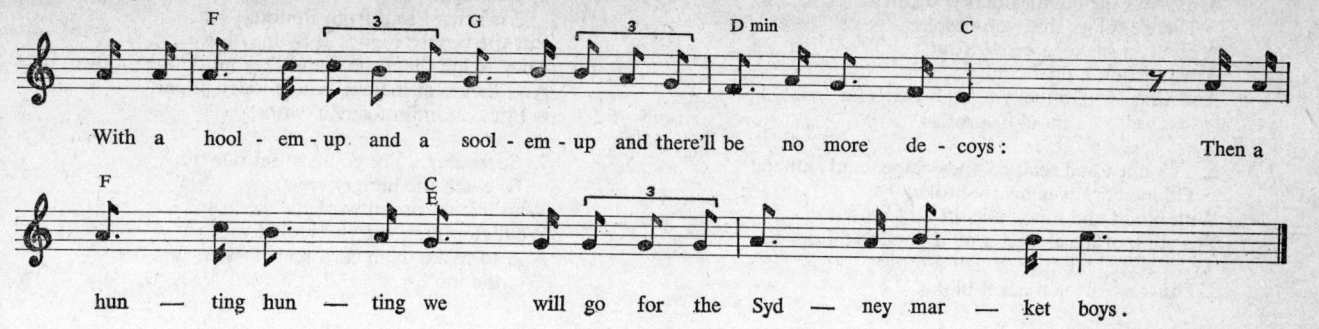

With a hool-em-up and a sool-em-up and there'll be no more de-coys: Then a hun-ting hun-ting we will go for the Syd-ney mar-ket boys.

1. I read about the fortunes that
   The rabbiters make outback –
The sporting life, and the lairy tales
Of prices fetched at Sydney sales,
So I started out across New South Wales
   On the roving rabbiters' track.

Chorus: With a hool-em-up and a sool-em-up
   And the fool-em-up decoys,
The men who scalp the rabbiters
Are the Sydney market boys.

2. A free and independent life,
   A life of simple joys –
I camped beneath an old belar,
And me tucker was mostly fried galah,
And I trapped 'em near and I trapped 'em far
   For the Sydney market boys.

3. I poisoned out at Hillston
   And I trapped at Gundagai;
I followed 'em over creeks and bogs,
And chopped 'em out of hollow logs,
And tailed 'em up with yelping dogs
   Way back of Boggabri.

4. Besides the bunnies that you catch
   There's things that you despise –
A hawk, a snake, a crow, a rat,
A bandicoot, a tiger cat,
And when you're lucky a lamb that's fat
   Is a welcome enough surprise.

5. I skinned and scalped and scalped and skinned
   Till me back was nearly broke,
With blood and muck all stiff and brown
The stink of me clothes would knock you down,
And I slaved all day for half a crown
   For the Sydney market bloke.

6. I thought I'ld get a snifter cheque
   For skins I sent from Bourke,
But the broker rogues at Sydney town
They weigh them short and they grade them down,
And they sent me back three lousy pound
   For a month of slavin' work.

7. Some day we're going to set our traps
   To catch the hungry crew
Who live on useful workers' sweat –
We'll stop their thievin' racket yet,
And to make them earn their tucker, you bet,
   Is the job for me and you.

Last Chorus: With a hool-em-up and a sool-em-up,
   And there'll be no more decoys;
Then a-hunting, hunting we will go
   For the Sydney market boys.

CANE KILLED ABEL

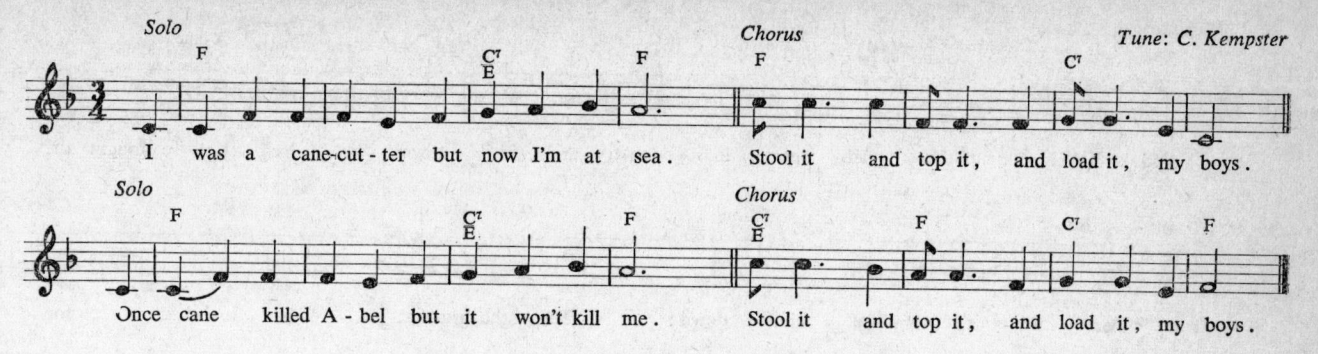

Tune: C. Kempster

1. SOLO: I was a cane cutter, but now I'm at sea,
   CHORUS: Stool it, and top it, and load it, my boys.
   SOLO: Once cane killed Abel, but it won't kill me,
   CHORUS: Stool it, and top it, and load it, my boys.

(*Solo lines only*)

2. There was an old seaman who sang this refrain,
He stood to the bar and he filled up again.

3. I rose every morning about half past three,
To cook me my breakfast, my dinner and tea.

4. I worked very hard until I went to sea,
Once cane killed Abel, and it almost killed me.

(*Repeat verse* 1 ad lib.)

THE DEATH OF NED KELLY

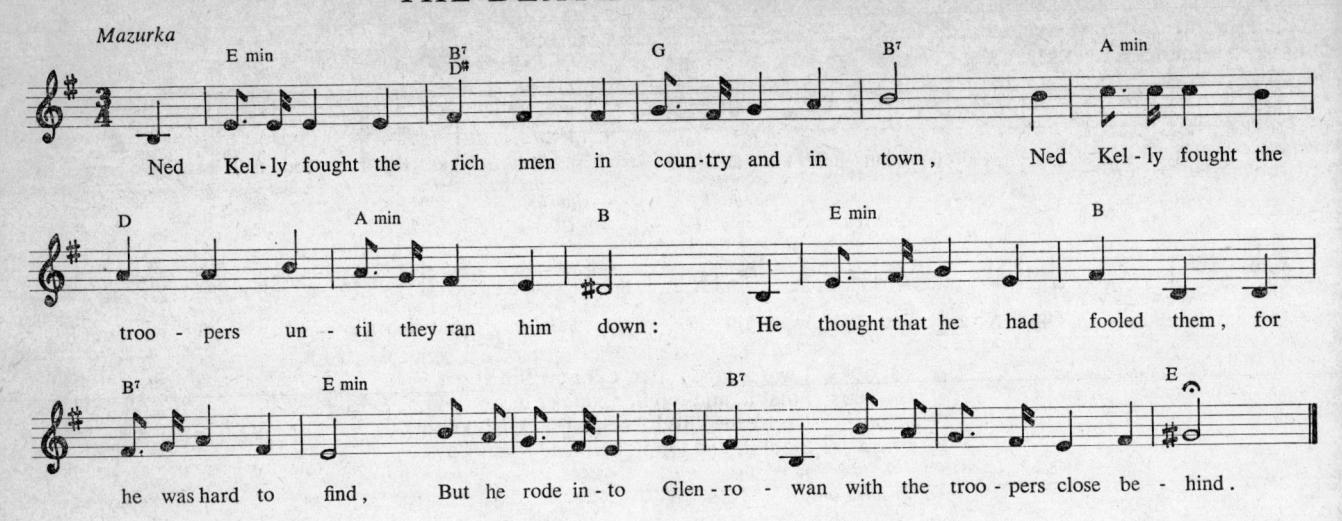

Mazurka

Ned Kel-ly fought the rich men in coun-try and in town, Ned Kel-ly fought the troo-pers un-til they ran him down: He thought that he had fooled them, for he was hard to find, But he rode in-to Glen-ro-wan with the troo-pers close be-hind.

1. Ned Kelly fought the rich men in country and in town,
Ned Kelly fought the troopers until they ran him down;
He thought that he had fooled them, for he was hard to find,
But he rode into Glenrowan with the troopers close behind.

2. 'Come out of that, Ned Kelly,' the head zarucker calls,
'Come out and leave your shelter, or we'll shoot it full of holes.'
'If you'd take me,' says Kelly, 'that's not the speech to use;
I've lived to spite your order, I'll die the way I choose!'

3. 'Come out of that, Ned Kelly, you done a lawless thing;
You robbed and fought the squatters, Ned Kelly, you must swing.'
'If those who rob,' says Kelly, 'are all condemned to die,
You had better hang the squatters; for they've stolen more than I.'

4. 'You'd best come out, Ned Kelly, you done the Government wrong,
For you held up the coaches that bring the gold along.'
'Go tell your boss,' says Kelly, 'who lets the rich go free,
That your bloody rich man's government will never govern me.'

5. They burned the roof above him, they fired the walls about,
And head to foot in armour Ned Kelly stumbled out;
Although his guns were empty he made them turn and flee,
But one came in behind him and shot him in the knee.

6. And so they took Ned Kelly and hanged him in the jail,
For he fought singlehanded although in iron mail.
And no man singlehanded can hope to break the bars;
It's a thousand like Ned Kelly who'll hoist the flag of stars.

ANDY'S GONE WITH CATTLE

Our Andy's gone with cattle now, our hearts are out of order. With Drought he's gone to battle now across the Queensland border. He's left us in dejection now; our thoughts with him are roving, It's dull on this selection now since Andy went a-droving.

1. Our Andy's gone with cattle now ... our hearts are out of order ...
With drought he's gone to battle now across the Queensland border.
He's left us in dejection now; our thoughts with him are roving;
It's dull on this selection now, since Andy went a-droving.

2. Who now shall wear the cheerful face in times when things are slackest?
And who shall whistle round the place when Fortune frowns her blackest?
And who shall cheek the squatter now, when he comes round us snarling?
His tongue is growing hotter now, since Andy crossed the Darling.

3. Oh may the showers in torrents fall, and all the tanks run over;
And may the grass grow green and tall in pathways of the drover;
And may good angels send the rain on desert stretches sandy,
And when the summer comes again, God grant it brings us Andy.

NOTES

THE COMMISSIONER, by Robert Lowe, later Viscount Sherbrooke.

Published in *Poems of a Life* (1884) but undoubtedly written before 1850. Robert Lowe was a likeable firebrand who spent his colonial term in fierce altercation with Governor Gipps. An anonymous epitaph on him is quoted sometimes:

> Here lies poor old Robert Lowe.
> Where he's gone to I don't know:
> If to the realms of peace and love,
> Then farewell happiness above!
> If, maybe, to the lower level,
> We can't congratulate the devil.

The tune is Scottish: 'Bonny Dundee'.

THE BROKEN-DOWN SQUATTER, by Charles Flower.

The brothers Flower, Charles and Horace, seem to have been prolific song-writers in the 1880s-90s. They were Queenslanders and station-owners, not by any means professional poets or musicians, but standing high in the amateur class. Some of their songs use American 'minstrel' tunes, others well known English tunes. The tune given here, taken down from the singing of the famous 'Hoop-iron Jack' Lee, of Auburn, New South Wales, appeared in *Singabout*, Vol. 2, No. 2. It apparently derives from the original tune to which Flower wrote his words, 'It's a Fine Hunting Day'. Anderson gives the latter. Palmer and Sutherland give another tune with no more than slight similarity.

Charles Flower's manuscripts have been collected and presented to the Oxley Library in Brisbane by W. N. Scott.

BILLYGOAT OVERLAND; TRAVELLING DOWN THE CASTLEREAGH; WALTZING MATILDA

By A. B. Paterson, 'The Banjo', and reprinted by courtesy of The Endeavour Press and Angus and Robertson Ltd.

Here are three songs which have gone into oral currency by three different routes. 'Billygoat Overland' has attached itself to 'The Lincolnshire Poacher'. 'Travelling Down the Castlereagh' simply grew or secreted its own tunes: there are two that have been collected by the Sydney Bush Music Club, and two more in the *Queensland Pocket Songbook*, apart from professional settings by Lavater, Truman, and Vuillaume. This one was first collected by Geoff Wills, and has since been given to me by Mr Hines, Donald, Victoria, who tells me that it was the one generally heard in his youth some forty years ago.

Paterson himself said that he wrote the words of 'Waltzing Matilda' to fit a tune played to him by Miss Christina Macpherson at Dagworth homestead, near Winton, Queensland, in 1895. Mr Sydney May in his book, *The Story of Waltzing Matilda*, makes out a very good case for this tune having been 'Bonny Wood of Craigielea', perhaps imperfectly memorized.

The Marie Cowan version given here preserves a strong resemblance to 'Craigielea', but does not adhere strictly to Paterson's words. The alternative tune, given to me by John O'Neill of Buderim, Queensland, does not resemble 'Craigielea' but does preserve Paterson's text.

More research is needed into the origins of both versions, and into the connexion (if any) of 'Craigielea' with an English song, said to be of seventeenth-century origin, called 'The Bold Fusilier'. I have put forward a hypothetical solution of some of the discrep-

175

ancies in my book *Who Wrote the Ballads?*, but this may well become obsolete when Mr Oscar Mendelsohn and Mr Harry Pearce publish the results of their present researches.

THE SHEARER'S DREAM; FREEDOM ON THE WALLABY; ANDY'S GONE WITH CATTLE, by Henry Lawson.

The facts about Lawson's songs are harder to be sure about than in the case of Paterson. This particular tune to 'The Shearer's Dream' was given to the Queensland Folklore Society by E. Loughlin, Dirranbandi; a different tune is given in *Singabout*, Vol. 2, No. 4, and in Anderson's *Colonial Ballads*, second edition. The words may be traditional, 'arr. and pub. Lawson', or may be pure Lawson. 'Freedom on the Wallaby' was printed in 1891, and is included in *The Men Who Made Australia*, edited by Majorie Pizer and published by the Australasian Book Society. Its tune came drifting down from the Townsville area after the war, and is also used for the ballad 'Australia's On the Wallaby'. Another tune is given in *Singabout*, Vol. 1, No. 2.

'Andy's Gone With Cattle' is the poem by which Lawson is so well known to children, because it has been included in many school anthologies. The tune is the one I learnt as a boy, and published in *Bandicoot Ballads*; Mrs Webb whom I have quoted before, confirms my impression that it is fairly old. Technically, it seems to belong to the James Hook period, and may have been a London pleasure garden song originally.

THE RABBITER

By Stan Wakefield (1906-62). No less an amateur than the Flower brothers, Wakefield composed both words and music of several songs during his roving life. His style is natural in the best sense, and completely free of literary affectation. Wakefield's own notes on this song are as follows: '*Decoy*: lure used by rabbit-poisoners; newspaper stories about "fortunes" made at rabbiting. *Hool, sool*: cry of encouragement to hunting-dogs; newspapers urging unemployed to earn profits for wealthy skin-dealers'. Text second tune from *Singabout*, Vol. 1, No. 2.

CANE KILLED ABEL

By Merv Lilley, music by Chris Kempster. Merv Lilley (b.1920) is another unprofessional poet who stands very close to folksong. Though the ships on which he served were all steamers, his verses retain the shape as well as the vigour of the old chanties.

From *Singabout*, Vol. 1, No. 1.

THE DEATH OF NED KELLY

By J.S. Manifold (b.1915). I wrote this one perfectly unselfconsciously and long before I became aware that a 'scientific' approach to folksong was desirable. All I had to go on in the first place was one incomplete verse and the traditional tune:

You've heard about Glenrowan, you've heard of Buckaroo;
It was there they caught Ned Kelly, the same I'll tell to you.

I completed the ballad to my own satisfaction, and sang it a good deal in an informal way. Then people began to sing it back to me, and in a weak moment I yielded to persuasion and printed it as a *Bandicoot Ballad*. Certainly I had no intention of passing off my own work as traditional – you will find the verses printed as my own in *The Death of Ned Kelly and Other Ballads*, London, 1941 – but I did and still do think that the tune needed to be preserved.

BOOKS THAT GIVE THE BACKGROUND

Part I

Ingleton, G.C. – *True Patriots All*, Sydney: Angus & Robertson, 1952.

Part II

Anderson, Hugh – *Colonial Minstrel*, Melbourne: Cheshire, 1960.

Part III

Meredith, John – *The Wild Colonial Boy: The Life and Times of Jack Donahoe, 1808-30*, Sydney: The Wentworth Press, 1960. Clune, Frank – *Wild Colonial Boys*, Sydney: Angus & Robertson, 1948. Brown, Max – *Australian Son: The Story of Ned Kelly*, Melbourne: Georgian House, 1948.

Part IV

Paterson, A.B. – *An Outback Marriage*, Sydney: Angus & Robertson, 1906. Collins, Tom – *Such is Life*, Sydney: The Bulletin Press, 1903. Phillips, A.A. – 'The Democratic Theme' (in *The Australian Tradition*), Melbourne: Cheshire, 1958. Kiddle, Margaret – *Men of Yesterday*, Melbourne: Melbourne University Press, 1961.

Part V

Ward, Russel – *The Australian Legend*, Melbourne: Oxford University Press, 1958. Palmer, Vance – *The Legend of the Nineties*, Melbourne: Melbourne University Press, 1954.

NOTES FOR ACCOMPANISTS

Guitarists are warned against trying to use cowboy, hill-billy, flamenco or dance-band techniques. The straight-forward German and Italian use of the instrument is all that is called for. The thumb is used on the bass strings only, except for special effect, and the plectrum is not used at all.

The appended tablature gives the *simplest* fingering of the chords used in this book. The vertical lines are the six strings of the guitar; the horizontal ones are the first five frets, seen from the front. Black dots indicate where the fingers go in stopping a string. White O's indicate strings that are to be struck 'open' or unstopped. It is normal to use the first (index) finger at first fret, second finger at second fret, third finger at third fret. The sixth string, the lowest E, is stopped with the thumb. When any departure from this rule is forced on you by the layout of the chord, place the 'normal' fingers first, and the 'abnormal' usage of the others will follow naturally.

Chord-letters superimposed on each other in the accompaniments show inversions of chords. Thus 'E min' over a 'G' means the chord of E-minor with its 'G' in the bass: 'G' over 'B' means a G-major chord with its 'B' in the bass. Players of four-stringed instruments ignore the lower letter in these cases, and players of the bass-guitar, double-bass, or other instruments that provide no chord, ignore the upper letter.

A letter followed by a small 'x' means bass-note only, without chord.

TABLE OF GUITAR CHORDS (1st Position) USED IN THIS BOOK

Minor chords	Major chords	Dominant-seventh chords
F♯ min	E	B⁷ — Easier in 1st inversion as B⁷/D♯
B min	A	E⁷
E min	D	A⁷
A min	G	D⁷
D min	C	G⁷
G min	F	C⁷
	B♭ — Easier in 1st inversion as B♭/D	

INDEX OF FIRST LINES

	page
A noble whale ship and commander	20
A sergeant and three constables rode out from Mansfield town	72
A strapping young stockman lay dying	83
A young man left his native town	42
All you on emigration bent	31
As I came down through Conroy's Gap	139
As I went to Dalby, upon a market day	97
Australia's a big country	167
Be ye stockmen or no, to my story give ear	86
Come all ye lads of the droving days, ye gentlemen unafraid	157
Come all you gallant poaching boys that ramble free of care	15
Come all you Lachlan men, and a sorrowful tale I'll tell	61
Come all you sons of liberty and listen to my tale	57
Come all you young Australians, and hear what did befall	63
Come Stumpy, old man, we must shift while we can	155
Farewell and adieu to you Brisbane ladies	121
Farewell and adieu to you, sweet Brisbane ladies	123
Farewell my home in Greta, my sister Kate farewell	67
Farewell to old England for ever	22
Frank Gardiner he is caught at last, he lies in Sydney gaol	59
Hark, hark the dogs are barking! my love, I must away	133
Humping old bluey, it is a stale game	142

	page
I draw for Speckle's Mill, bullocky-O, bullocky-O	137
I come from the South, and my name it's Field	118
I read about the fortunes that	169
I was a cane cutter, but now I'm at sea	171
If you'll but listen, a sorrowful tale I'll tell	51
I'm a broke alluvial miner, who's been used his cup to drain	101
I'm only a backblocks shearer, as easily can be seen	129
I'm travelling down the Castlereagh, and I'm a station hand	159
It was just about a year ago, as near as I can guess	41
I've been a few miles, I've crossed a few stiles	96
I've been a wild rover this many a year	147
I've been many years a shearer, and fancied I could shear	127
I've shore at Burrabogie, and I've shore at Toganmain	135
Jacky-Jacky was a smart young fellow	95
My name is Ben Hall, from Murrurundi I came	47
My name is Edward Kelly, I'm honoured vastly well	65
Nae lark in transport mounts the sky	23
Ned Kelly fought the rich men in country and in town	173
Now, all you blokes, take my advice and do your daily toil	105
O hark the dogs are barking, love, I can no longer stay	131
O listen for a moment lads, and hear me tell my tale	13
Oh, gather round, you sailor boys, and listen to my song	7
Oh, I dreamt I shore in a shearin'-shed, and it was a dream of joy	165
Oh, I'm sixteen thousand miles from home	33

179

	page
Oh, I've just come from Sydney, across the range of mountains	143
Oh, my name is Bob the Swagman, and I'll have you understand	89
Oh, South Australia's my native home	4
Oh, the shearing is all over and the wool is coming down	141
Oh, the sun went down, and the moon advanced	24
Oh, there once was a swagman camped in a billabong	163
Oh, who hasn't heard of Euabalong Ball	99
Old Black Alice are my name, Wellshot are my station	93
Once a jolly swagman camp'd by a billabong	161
One night when travelling sheep, my companions lay asleep	125
One Sunday morning as I went walking, by Brisbane waters I chanced to stray	18
Our Andy's gone with cattle now . . . our hearts are out of order	174
Sing ho, for a brave and gallant ship	9
Sure, Paddy dear, and did you hear the news that's going round	74
The commissioner bet me a pony – I won	153
The miner he goes and changes his clothes	43
The old man came to the men's hut door	81
The song I'm going to sing to you will not detain you long	91

	page
The sweet-scented wattle sheds perfume around	145
The wind is fair and free, my boys	39
There was a valiant highwayman of courage and renown	49
There was a wild colonial youth, Jack Doolan was his name	54
There's a long green gully on the Eumerella shore	107
There's a song in my heart for the one I love best	5
There's a trade you all know well	116
'Twas an Inglewood cocky of whom I've been told	109
'Twas in the city of London	11
When first I left Old Ireland's shore, the yarns that we were told	37
When first I took the Western track, 'twas many years ago	138
When I first arrived at Quirindi, those girls they jumped with joy	117
When I was at home I was down on my luck	35
When shearing comes, lay down your drums	108
You lads and lasses all attend to me	19
Ye sons of Australia forget not your braves	68
Ye sons of industry, to you I belong	103